Benito Mussolini

Mussolini addresses the Fascist faithful

Anthony L. Cardoza

Loyola University Chicago

Benito Mussolini

The First Fascist

New York San Francisco Boston
London Toronto Sydney Tokyo Singapore Madrid
Mexico City Munich Paris Cape Town Hong Kong Montreal

Cover Designer: Laura Shaw
Cover Photo: © Corbis, Inc.

ISBN 0–321–36580-1

To my son, Michael

Contents

Author's Preface

The Italian dictator, Benito Mussolini, can justly lay claim to a number of firsts. As the charismatic founder and leader of the world's first Fascist regime, he provided the prototype for a new kind of populist dictator that inspired Adolf Hitler and others who dominated the global stage during first half of the twentieth century. In his role as the all-knowing and all-powerful "Duce" (*Dew*-chay) or "Captain" of Italy, he also was the first political figure to make extensive use of modern mass media to construct an image of the leader that captured the public imagination. Mussolini's magnetic physical presence made him the living embodiment of fascism's values and the model for the strong and virile "new fascist man" that his regime relentlessly glorified in print, art, architecture, radio, and films. Accordingly, the Duce stands out as one of the pioneers of a new culture of "celebrity" that spread rapidly from the world of politics to sports and entertainment in the second half of the twentieth century. Much like some of our contemporary celebrities, however, he ultimately fell victim to his own image-making. When the Duce and the regime he personified failed in wartime to live up to the expectations he had created, his allies abandoned him, the Italian public turned on him, and a wave of popular revulsion drove him from power and led to his ignominious demise.

Benito Mussolini is ideally suited to the Weekend Biography series, with its emphasis on the role of exceptional individuals who shaped the course of history. Mussolini's turbulent life intersected with most of the major developments in Europe's "Age of Catastrophe" from 1914 to 1945. Mussolini first gained the public's attention as a fire-breathing propagandist of Italy's "revolutionary" left, but he abruptly abandoned the cause of international socialism in 1914, only to reinvent himself the next year as an aggressive nationalist in the campaign for Italian intervention in World War I. In the chaotic postwar years, Mussolini moved to the forefront of national political life once again as the key protagonist in the rise and triumph of fascism, a violently nationalistic, anticommunist, and antidemocratic mass movement. Without his combination of tactical skills, ruthlessness, and charisma, it is hard to imagine the Fascists coming to power, let alone ruling Italy for more than two decades. While he borrowed ideas, rituals, and methods from a variety of sources, Mussolini was unquestionably the principal architect, chief interpreter, and dominant figure of the Italian Fascist dictatorship.

Mussolini's historical importance extended beyond the borders of his own country. His conquest of power in Italy made him an inspiration to Fascist movements elsewhere and transformed him into one of the most well-known public figures in the world by the early 1930s. More important, as dictator of a self-proclaimed "totalitarian" state and Hitler's principal ally, Mussolini played a direct role in a series of larger European and global crises associated with the Great Depression, imperial expansion, and military aggression. His life culminated fittingly in World War II and the death throes of the European world order.

At the same time, Mussolini's personality and love of flamboyant rhetoric, gestures, and actions lend themselves to a biography that uses personal drama to illustrate larger themes in a historical context. The Duce was not simply the invention of a public relations campaign. Mussolini led an exciting life filled with dramatic moments, romantic escapades, and harrowing escapes that offer an abundance of good stories to enliven the narrative and hold the reader's attention.

Finally, the contradictions and complexities of Mussolini's political career and personality provide an excellent opportunity to reveal significant issues of historical interpretation. There is still much disagreement among scholars about the Duce and his place in the history of Europe in the twentieth century. Historians and political commentators have variously depicted him as an opportunistic scoundrel, failed dictator, modernizing autocrat, genuine revolutionary, and dynamic new leader. While my own assessment of the man and his achievements is highly critical, the final chapter on his legacy discusses scholarly disagreements and debates about Mussolini in order to give readers a glimpse into the ways historians have studied and explained the Duce. Readers interested in finding additional information on Mussolini can consult "A Note on the Sources," which details the reading I did in preparing the book.

A number of individuals and institutions aided me in the preparation of this book. I wish, first of all, to acknowledge Peter N. Stearns for inviting to me to participate in the Weekend Biography series. I must also record my gratitude to Loyola University Chicago for a paid leave of absence in 2003 that allowed me to do much of the writing on the book. Much as in the past, the advice, criticism, and friendship of Professor Alexander

De Grand of North Carolina State University have been of inestimable value to me in the period of writing and revision of the manuscript. My warmest thanks are due to him, Professor R. J. B. Bosworth of the University of Western Austria, and Professor Stearns for their insightful readings of earlier drafts. Erika Gutierrez and Janet Lanphier have been patient and supportive editors, while Stephanie Ricotta did a superb job of editing the final version of the manuscript. A final word of appreciation goes to my wife, Catherine Mardikes, and our son, Michael, to whom this book is dedicated.

ANTHONY L. CARDOZA

Benito Mussolini

I

Rebel Without a Cause

1883–1910

Italy, the country that Benito Mussolini would rule over in the twentieth century, did not emerge as a unified state until the early 1860s. It was largely the creation of a small but wealthy group of landed gentlemen who carried to completion Italy's *Risorgimento,* or "Resurrection," a half-century-long campaign for national unification. This elite skillfully exploited divisions among the great powers of Europe and a wave of local revolts on the Italian peninsula to bring together an extremely diverse collection of regional states and communities in the years between 1859 and 1870. Although the new governing class succeeded in establishing a liberal political system with a constitution, representative institutions, and a limited monarchy, they enjoyed little popular support and had to contend with recurring revolts and rebellions. At the same time, the Italian state faced fierce opposition from the Roman Catholic Church. Church leaders had ruled one of the old states, but lost their power in 1861 when their territories were incorporated into the newly unified Italy. Pius IX, the pope at the time, and his immediate successors steadfastly denied recognition to the national state. These political challenges accentuated the difficulties this fragile regime had to face in ruling over a poor, largely illiterate, agricultural society that lacked decent means of communications, an integrated national economy, or any real sense of a larger collective identity.

At the same time, the Italian state confronted enormous challenges in foreign policy. From the outset, the country's economic and military weakness unavoidably reduced Italy's diplomatic weight and made it the "least" of the great powers of Europe. To make matters worse, the creation of the new nation antagonized two important bordering states, Austria-Hungary and France, who had treated the Italian peninsula as their own zones of influence in the past. Moreover, Italy's long, exposed coastline made her national security and colonial aspirations in North Africa dependent upon friendly relations with Great Britain, the leading naval power in the Mediterranean. These circumstances forced the new nation to pursue a foreign policy that oscillated between the rival

Benito at the age of fourteen

great powers in order to avoid dangerous isolation without creating powerful enemies.

To solidify their rule, Italy's leaders developed a system of rule that limited voting rights and relied on various forms of corruption, pressure, and intimidation to win elections and keep their adversaries out of politics even as the country descended into a worldwide agricultural depression in the last decades of the century. By the 1880s, popular discontent against this narrowly based state began to take organized form with urban and rural workers converting to the cause of socialism or else joining the new Catholic labor

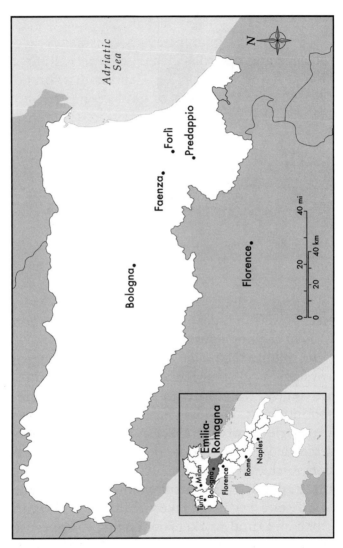

Important sites in Mussolini's early years in Emilia-Romagna

movement. The government of the era responded with repression, guaranteeing a constant cycle of violence and disorder in Italian society. Repression at home went hand-in-hand with efforts to develop a foreign policy of prestige in the 1880s and 1890s based on an alliance with the central powers, Germany and Austria-Hungary, and colonial expansion on the African continent. This policy, however, brought Italy into conflict with France in North Africa and culminated in the humiliating defeat of the Italian army by the Ethiopians at the Battle of Adowa in 1896.

In a country like Italy in the 1880s, few would have anticipated Mussolini's extraordinary career on the basis of his family background and early life. Benito Amilcare Andrea Mussolini entered the world on a Sunday afternoon, July 29, 1883, in a small house near the village of Predappio, ten miles from the nearest town of Forlì in the east central region of the Romagna, the first son of Alessandro Mussolini and his wife, Rosa Maltoni. He was joined eighteen months later by a younger brother, Arnaldo, who was followed by a sister, Edvige, in 1888. The two brothers, in particular, developed a very close relationship until Arnaldo's premature death in 1931. Later in life, Mussolini liked to emphasize his family's humble origins and poverty. As he often recollected, the family lived in a sparsely furnished two-room cottage attached to his mother's school, where she was a teacher. Benito and his brother shared a bed in a room that also served as the kitchen and made do with a diet that included meat only once a week. By the standards of the time, though, the Mussolinis were relatively comfortable compared to their neighbors in the village. They could afford to, for instance, have plenty of books in the house, pay for domestic help, and allow the two boys to remain in school until the age of eighteen.

Mussolini's parents, however, possessed divergent views of the world, which may have contributed to some of the confusion and contradictions in his ideas. His father came from a family of small peasant landholders who had fallen on hard times. Both his father and grandfather, Luigi, were from the Romagna, a relatively poor region with a long tradition of political violence and rebelliousness. In the nineteenth century the region became a hotbed of anti-clerical republicanism, anarchism, and international socialism under the rule of the pope in Rome. Luigi, who lost the family farm and worked as a hired hand, took part in the political disturbances of the late 1840s and spent time in papal jails. Alessandro, a self-educated blacksmith by trade, was a well-known local revolutionary figure. He devoted himself to an anarchistic brand of socialism that favored violent direct action over peaceful change and legal reforms. Alessandro's allegiances found fitting expression in the christening of his first son, whom he had named after the Mexican revolutionary Benito Juarez and two prominent Romagnolo socialists, Amilcare Cipriani and Andrea Costa. Benito's mother, Rosa Maltoni, came from a more affluent and respectable family. Her father, a veterinarian and local landowner, had the means to provide her with some formal education; she received a diploma as an elementary school teacher and took a post near Predappio where she met her future husband. In sharp contrast to the anticlerical Alessandro, Rosa was a pious Catholic who insisted on a religious ceremony when they wed in 1882, had all her children baptized, and took them to church every Sunday. Such a contrasting background seems particularly appropriate for Mussolini, a man who began his political career as a brutally outspoken adversary of Catholicism and ended by becoming the great ally of the papacy in Italy.

By all accounts, even as a young boy Benito displayed a violence and restlessness that remained the hallmarks of his political style and methods throughout his life. He himself later recalled that he was "a pugnacious and violent kid," boasting years later how "many of my playmates still carry on their heads the signs of my stones." According to other accounts, he commanded a gang of boys who raided local farms and was a bully who provoked fights at the drop of a hat, plucked live chickens, and pinched people in church until they cried. On at least two occasions, Benito's behavior got him into serious trouble. At the age of nine, his mother insisted, over his father's reservations, that he be sent off to a boarding school run by the Salesian Brothers, a Catholic religious order, in Faenza, a city near Forlì. Conflicts with the priests and other students over politics, religion, and social class made the experience a miserable one for the boy. Benito brought this educational experiment to an abrupt end two years later when he stabbed one of his classmates in the hand and was expelled from the school. More fighting and another stabbing incident led to two suspensions from his next boarding school, which he continued to attend as a day student.

Despite these behavioral problems, Mussolini also had a bookish side and read widely in his family's well-stocked library. He proved an able student in his teen years with a variety of extracurricular activities. In high school he displayed a good memory, excelled in language, literature, and history, and developed an enduring interest in music. He also provided the first indications of his exceptional oratorical skills in this period. In 1901 his school selected him to give a public address, commemorating the death of the great Italian composer Giuseppe Verdi, for which he received favorable attention in the regional press. Of course, life was not all brawling and studying for the young man. A former school-mate recalled that Benito was a passionate and athletic dancer, more interested in girls than pol-itics. After he lost his virginity in a house of prostitution in Forlì during the 1899–1900 school year, Benito embarked upon what would become a lifelong career of sexual conquests that, one writer calculated, eventually numbered over four hundred women, included several mistresses, and produced various illegitimate children.

By the time of his graduation in 1901, then, Mussolini already manifested certain personality traits that would distinguish him in his subsequent public life. As he conceded to a German journalist decades later, "Anyone closely acquainted with me at that time could have already recognized when I was sixteen what I now am, with all the light and shade." His former classmates seemed to concur with this mixed judgment. On the one hand, they remembered a proud, bright, intense, and ambi-tious young man. On the other hand, they also saw in him a rebellious, violence-prone loner with an exalted sense of his own importance and no close friends, the sort of person who preferred dominance and power to companionship in his dealings with members of both sexes.

At the dawn of the twentieth century, such qualities did not seem to afford many conventional career opportunities for a provincial young Italian of modest means and without connections. Mussolini displayed little sense of direction or commitment that might have improved these limited prospects for several years after he left school. Instead he led a rather aimless, nomadic, bohemian existence that entailed frequent moves, no stable employment, and scandalous affairs, as well as run-ins with the authorities.

Initially, Mussolini attempted to follow in the footsteps of his mother by pursuing a career as an elementary school teacher. Between 1902 and 1908, he held three different teaching positions, each for a brief duration. In February 1902, he took his first post as a substitute teacher in a village some one hundred kilometers from home. At the end of the semester, however, the school did not renew his contract after he clashed with parents, spent excessive time in the local bars, and had an adulterous affair with the wife of a local soldier off on active duty. Four years later, he took another teaching job in a village near the Italian border with Austria, where he encountered many of the same problems. Mussolini had difficulty maintaining order in the classroom and offended the devoutly Catholic local population with his crude anti-clerical opinions. To make matters worse, he once again had an affair with a local married woman. When the woman's husband confronted him, Benito later boasted, the two men got into a fight, in which "the husband naturally got the worst of it, being older and weaker than me." Not surprisingly, his contract was not renewed at the end of the summer of 1907. After Mussolini passed an exam in French in November that qualified him to teach in secondary schools, he took his last teaching position at a private Catholic middle school in Oneglia on the Italian Riviera in the spring of 1908, but once again the job ended at the end of the semester.

Mussolini's most important formative experiences actually took place during an interlude from 1902 to 1904 when he lived in Switzerland. A number of factors led the nineteen-year-old to seek his fortune by emigrating abroad in the summer of 1902: difficulties finding work, a spirit of adventure and rebelliousness, a reluctance to have to move back to his parents' home, and a general dislike for the daily grind of teaching. At first, Benito's life as an immigrant seemed to offer little more than misery and humiliation. Grueling manual labor, nights spent sleeping on park benches or in flophouses, hunger, illness, and loneliness all made up the tapestry of his early days away from Italy.

Nonetheless, his time in Switzerland proved to be an invaluable voyage of self-discovery for the young man. To begin with, Benito realized right away that he could not live and work like ordinary people. He certainly was temperamentally unsuited to the type of hard, low-paying, manual labor performed by most other Italian emigrants, as he made abundantly clear in a letter to a friend:

> I found work and on Monday morning, the 14th, I began. Eleven hours' work a day, thirty-two centimes an hour. I made one hundred and twenty-one trips with a hand-barrow full of stones up to the second floor of a batiment in process of construction. In the evening, the muscles of my arms were swollen. I ate some potatoes baked in ashes. At five on Tuesday, I awoke and returned to work. I chafed with the terrible rage of the powerless. The boss was making me mad . . . . Saturday evening came. I told the boss that I intended to leave and that therefore he should pay me . . . . With ill-disguised rage, he threw into my hands twenty lire and some centimes, saying: "Here is your pay and it is stolen." I stood petrified. What should I have done to him? Kill him? What did I do to him? Nothing. Why? Because I was hungry and had no shoes.

In the following months, Mussolini took a variety of other jobs, but all of them were temporary. In any case, such work became less and less important to the young man. His evident aversion to manual labor, hatred of authority, and intellectual pretensions drew him to his first true callings: rabble-rousing journalism and radical politics.

Mussolini soon discovered his father's political legacy; his own strong personality, educational background, and gifts for public speaking and writing made him particularly well suited to the roles of labor organizer and promoter of socialist ideas among the Italian immigrant workers in Switzerland. Within weeks of his arrival in that country, Mussolini wrote his first article for a local socialist newspaper and later assumed the post of secretary of the Italian bricklayers' union in Berne. Despite his youth and lack of experience, the nineteen-year-old Benito proved a dynamic and energetic organizer and strike leader who rapidly developed a following among his fellow Italian emigrants. Above all, he showed a particular talent for inflammatory speeches that played on the resentments of his working-class audiences and inspired them to action. His local fame grew as he traveled extensively in 1902 and 1903, addressing rallies and attending socialist labor meetings throughout Switzerland. During the same period, Mussolini displayed real prowess as a partisan journalist, skilled at coming up with dramatic headlines and catchy slogans. He not only began to write frequently for the Italian socialist weekly paper in Switzerland, but he also published articles for socialist weeklies in New York and Milan. To bolster his standing as a journalist and intellectual, Mussolini studied German and French and embarked upon an ambitious reading project to broaden his knowledge of the leading thinkers of the day. By 1904, his work as a labor organizer, propagandist, and fledgling intellectual received recognition from the press back in Italy. The correspondent in Geneva for the Roman newspaper *La Tribuna* went so far as to call him the "great duce" or leader of the local socialist movement, the first time the term became attached to his name.

These activities soon attracted the attention of both Swiss authorities and influential figures within the Italian socialist movement. For their part, the authorities viewed the young man as a dangerous troublemaker who fomented violence, and they treated him accordingly. In the summer of 1903, the police in Berne briefly jailed Mussolini for his role in a carpenters' strike before expelling him from the canton, the first of several arrests and expulsions during the next year and a half. Decades later, the Duce treated as a badge of honor this period when he "tasted prison in various countries—eleven times in all." More importantly, Mussolini's work as a labor organizer and journalist also brought him into contact with the leading revolutionary or maximalist Italian socialist, Giacinto Menotti Serrati, and his Russian friend Angelica Balabanoff, who lived in Switzerland at the time. By 1904 they had taken him under their wing and became his political mentors and most influential supporters within the Italian Socialist Party in the next decade. Fittingly, Benito and Angelica became lovers as well.

During his stay in Switzerland, Mussolini also began to articulate a set of basic ideas as well as a political style that would remain with him throughout his time in the ranks of socialism. From the outset, he identified himself exclusively with the most extreme, violent elements of the Italian movement. Like his father before him, Benito enthusiastically embraced the cause of revolutionary socialism and hostility to the Catholic church after 1902, describing himself as an "authoritarian communist." In common with most defenders of orthodox Marxist socialism of the era, he advocated direct action and violence by the workers to expropriate the propertied classes, abolish private property, and destroy the monarchical state as the bulwark of capitalism and imperialism. He combined these views with strong attacks on the Catholic church and the armed forces. Not surprisingly, he also viewed all moderate socialist groups who favored gradual reforms, democratic procedures, and parliamentary politics as bitter enemies.

What distinguished Mussolini from even his most ardent revolutionary comrades was not the clarity of his ideas so much as the rhetorical excesses and extremism of his speeches and writings. From the outset, he glorified violence as the most effective instrument of change, a stance that reflected his character and the traditions of his native Romagna. As he expressed it, "When all roads are closed, it is necessary to open a passage even at the cost of blood. Sometimes, vengeance for continued acts of infamy . . . is holy." This apology for violence provides insight into his other views. Mussolini the anti-monarchist, for example, denounced German Emperor William II as "the ridiculous Attila of the twentieth century" and the ruling family of Italy, the House of Savoy, as "bigots and reactionaries." He even went so far as to praise the man who had assassinated Italy's "imperialist sovereign" King Humbert I in 1900 and to ridicule the short stature and physical deformity of his successor, Victor Emanuel III. He also outdid his fellow socialists in the tone of his anti-clericalism by attacking not only the Catholic church as an institution, but also the moral philosophy of Jesus Christ that, in his view, led "to brutishness and cowardice and perpetuates misery." He embraced an equally extreme anti-militarism, depicting the armed forces as an agency of jingoist or warlike patriotism and openly calling for mass desertions by the soldiers as the "infallible means of destroying" it. In the short run, at least, Benito appeared to put his anti-militarism and anti-patriotism into practice. When his age group became eligible for obligatory military service in Italy in early 1904, he chose not to return home and instead became a draft dodger.

Despite the violence of his rhetoric and the extremism of his views, Mussolini was not singlemindedly and fanatically committed to his beliefs and their implementation like his German counterpart, Adolf Hitler. Rather he showed signs of a highly flexible approach to ideology and ideas. With all his pretensions to being a "socialist intellectual" familiar with the latest theories and cultural trends, Benito never was a coherent or deep political thinker. On the whole, he distrusted or was indifferent to political doctrines and preferred to treat ideas as instruments in his passionate thirst for action and power. He skillfully assimilated and echoed any current of thought that appealed to his confrontational temperament or reinforced his short-term political ambitions. He studded his speeches and writings with references to such diverse theorists and speculative thinkers as Karl Marx, Charles Darwin, Friedrich Nietzsche, Georges Sorel, and Vilfredo

Pareto. But their ideas represented little more than a series of intellectual acquisitions, which he superimposed on each other without apparent concern for their mutual inconsistencies and contradictions.

Mussolini eloquently demonstrated his ideological flexibility and his opportunism at the end of 1904 when he took advantage of the Italian government's general amnesty for draft dodgers to return home and perform his military service. For all his public attacks on the army and patriotism and his calls for mass desertions during his sojourn in Switzerland, Benito spent the next year and a half in the *bersaglieri*, an elite corps of the Italian army. In fact, all signs of his rebelliousness and hostility to authority seemingly vanished during these months. He did not hesitate to reject as dangerous adventures, for instance, proposals from socialist colleagues that he organize anti-military propaganda with the army. He told his commanding officer soon after his enlistment how he now wanted to do his "duties as a soldier and citizen . . . against the barbarians of the north" in order to "commemorate the heroes who cemented the unity of the Fatherland with their blood." In line with these words, he performed his military duties with discipline and zeal, embracing enthusiastically the army's male values and culture of patriotic violence.

Mussolini's retreat from socialist militancy may also have reflected traumas on the home front. Early in 1905, his mother, who had been in poor health, contracted meningitis and died at the age of 46. By some accounts, Benito took her passing very hard, begging her forgiveness on her deathbed for his past excesses and promising to mend his ways in the future. Whatever the truth of these stories, one thing is clear: In spite of his success as a socialist organizer and propagandist in Switzerland, he had not yet committed to a career in politics and journalism. In the wake of his mother's death, he seemed to opt instead for a life of more conventional respectability by returning to the teaching profession and by assuming a more responsible role in family matters after he had completed his military duties in September 1906. The following year he even promised local authorities in Forlì that he would abandon political activism altogether if they would expunge his police record.

Nonetheless, instability continued to characterize Mussolini's personal and professional lives. The path of the straight and narrow proved to be no match for the allure of new sexual adventures, gambling, and carousing in local bars. Mussolini's wild personal behavior, together with his predilection for anti-clerical tirades, cost him his second teaching job in a primary school in Tolmezzo on the northeastern border of Italy in the summer of

1907. After a brief stay at his home in Predappio, he took another post in a middle school in Oneglia on the Italian Riviera in early 1908, but this job also ended after a semester. By then, his interest in teaching had given way to a renewed enthusiasm for radical politics and journalism.

Indeed, politics reappeared on Mussolini's horizon already during his time in Oneglia. Here he began to collaborate with local socialists and took charge of their weekly paper, *La Lima*. He continued to act as a correspondent for the weekly upon his return to his father's new home in Forlì, where Alessandro had opened up a bar. Benito almost immediately became a center of controversy during a bitter local strike in mid-July. The police arrested him and he was convicted on charges of assault after he confronted and threatened to beat up a plant manager. Although he wound up serving 15 days in jail, he emerged as a local hero among the workers in Forlì and received tributes from the leftist press, including the national daily of the Italian Socialist party, *Avanti!* This notoriety and the support of his socialist mentors, Serrati and Balabanoff, landed him his first important political post. In the winter of 1908–1909, he took over as head of the socialist organization and editor of the party paper in Trent, the chief city of the Austrian-controlled border area of the Trentino, which was claimed by Italian nationalists. Once again, he displayed his talents for stirring speeches and violent polemics, especially against the Catholics, which brought him to the attention of the Austrian officials. He served jail time on charges of libel on at least two occasions, once for accusing three priests of sexual misconduct and a second time for calling another priest a rabid dog. Despite tensions between the German-speaking and Italian-speaking populations in Austria, Mussolini strongly opposed the claims of Italian nationalists to this "unreclaimed" area. In fact he insisted that the workers should be "anti-patriotic by definition and by necessity" in solidarity with the laboring classes everywhere, and he accused the supporters of the "bourgeois fatherland" of attempting "to cover up their own defense of privileges and of the riches of all exploiters with their empty patrioteering ideology." As in the past, Benito managed to combine radical politics with an equally frenetic personal life in Trent where he carried on simultaneous affairs with two women, one of whom gave birth to a child of his who died a few months later. After a number of other run-ins with the law, the Austrian authorities finally deported Mussolini in September 1909.

Despite the notoriety he had achieved in the Trentino, the twenty-six-year-old Mussolini remained unsure about what path he wanted to take in life. Certainly, a career in socialist politics was not a certainty as late as the winter of 1909–1910. Shortly after taking the post in Trent, he made this clear in a letter to a close friend: "As for my future, I have no fixed plans. I am living, as always, from hand to mouth. I have put advertisements in the newspapers, offering myself as a private teacher of French. If I succeed in living by this means, I shall give up the [party] secretaryship immediately." Upon his return to Forlì in the fall of 1909, Benito talked once again of emigrating abroad, perhaps even to the United States. During the same period, he applied unsuccessfully for a position as a journalist with a conservative daily paper in the city of Bologna, *Il Resto del Carlino*, a job that would have taken him far away from his old political allies on the left. Likewise, his continuing desire to be seen as an intellectual led him to praise enthusiastically fashionable thinkers whose nationalist and elitist views did not always mesh well with his ostensible convictions as a socialist and defender of the working classes.

Mussolini's ambivalence about a career in politics ended in 1910 as a result of major changes in his personal and professional lives. That year he embarked upon the most durable relationship of his life. Rachele Guidi was one of five daughters of a peasant widow who had moved in with

Benito's father, Alessandro, after the death of his wife in 1905. Seven years younger than Mussolini, Rachele came from even more modest circumstances and had few intellectual interests, but her lack of pretensions, her blonde hair, blue eyes, and stocky build evidently appealed to the young man. Benito started to court her before his departure for the Trentino in 1908. Despite his affairs with other women during his stay in Trent, the couple reunited on his return to Forlì over the opposition of Alessandro and her mother. Benito reportedly overcame such parental opposition to the relationship by threatening to shoot himself and Rachele. Early in 1910 they began to live together as socialist comrades or, as Mussolini put it, "without official sanctions, either civil or religious." Nine months later Rachele gave birth to a baby girl, Edda, the first of five children the couple would have over the next 19 years. While Mussolini never abandoned his predilection for keeping mistresses and indulging in casual sexual encounters with other women, Rachele remained a permanent fixture in his life. The two formalized their unconventional relationship with a civil ceremony in 1915, followed ten years later by a church wedding. In her role as his wife and the mother of his legitimate children, Rachele provided him with something that his German counterpart, Hitler, never enjoyed: the semblance of a normal family life. Benito's entry into parenthood came shortly before another major rite of passage, the death of his father. In November 1910, a partially paralyzed Alessandro passed away at the age of 56. As legend would have it, Benito vowed his eternal allegiance to the socialist cause at his father's grave. Whatever the truth of this legend, his new domestic situation coincided with a new stability in his work life.

In the second week of January 1910, Mussolini accepted posts as editor of the socialist weekly *La Lotta di Classe* and as secretary of the local chapter of the Socialist party in Forlì. In these dual roles, Mussolini lost no time displaying once again his rare gifts as journalist and public speaker. Working at a frenetic pace, he handled virtually all aspects of the paper and traveled around the province giving speeches to rally the faithful and recruit new converts on the days he was off. Much as in the past, he delighted in adopting the most extreme positions and employed a violent revolutionary rhetoric against his usual cast of conservative enemies: the Catholic church, monarchy, military establishment, nationalism, and parliamentary system. Thus, he denounced religion as "a gangrenous and shameful sore of superstition," the army as "a criminal organization designed to protect capitalism and bourgeois society," and the Italian national flag as "a rag to plant on a dunghill." Mussolini also opened up a second propagandistic battlefront on the left against the local republican political movement, which had long enjoyed a stronghold of support in Romagna and appealed to the same groups as the socialists. Against these competitors, he positioned himself as a defender of uncompromising intransigence and revolutionary direct action.

At the same time, Mussolini, as leader of the Forlì socialists, set out to remake the provincial party organization into the nucleus of a new type of revolutionary movement more suited to his temperament. Rejecting socialist traditions of mass organization, he attempted instead to forge a small cohesive group based on an idealistic and dedicated elite capable of leading the masses into battle. As he expressed it, "we prefer *quality* to *quantity*. To the obedient, resigned, stupid herd, which follows the shepherd and disperses at the first cry of wolves, we prefer the small, resolute, audacious nucleus which . . . knows what it wants and marches directly towards its goal."

The young socialist leader's style and extremist views made quite an impression in the province of Forlì and then in Romagna, a region long noted for its traditions of rebellion and political violence, and he quickly developed a growing following. While he failed to break the republican stranglehold over the province, he did manage to increase the number of local socialist sections and card-carrying members of the party in his first year. He was equally successful as a journalist; his editorial skills and lively articles dramatically boosted sales and subscriptions of *La Lotta di Classe*. As a result, he could boast in mid-1911 with some justification that few other electoral colleges in Italy had "such a large and cohesive bloc of socialist forces." Perhaps more importantly, Mussolini's own personal magnetism had played a major role in these successes. Contemporaries began to comment on his commanding presence, his oratorical brilliance, his dark blazing eyes, his dynamism, and his "extraordinary masculinity." At the age of 29, Mussolini had already established himself as the uncontested leader of the socialists in Forlì and had become a prominent figure in the local intellectual community.

Benito's status as a local hero in a provincial backwater, however, did not satisfy the young man's desire for attention, fame, and power. Even before he had consolidated his position in Forlì, he began to use his local power base as a launching pad to political prominence within the Socialist party at the national level. In the years 1910–1914, he found the ideal moment in Italy for his distinctive brand of revolutionary extremism. Indeed, his political message and style rapidly catapulted him to national prominence in those years. For the first, but not last, time in his life, Mussolini was the right man at the right place.

II

The Political Chameleon

1910–1919

By 1910 Italy had become a considerably more developed and powerful nation than it had been during Mussolini's childhood. Above all, in the first decade of the new century, the country experienced a period of unparalleled industrial growth and social progress. With the chemical, metallurgical, and engineering sectors leading the way, manufacturing production more than doubled and the annual rate of growth reached record highs in these years. Indeed, Italy enjoyed the greatest relative economic advance of any major European nation in the years from 1896 to 1908. The same period witnessed major changes in Italian society. Industrialization and falling death rates led to an increase in population that was accompanied by a steady movement from the countryside to the towns and cities. After decades of economic stagnation and misery, large numbers of Italians began to experience a real improvement in their standard of living, while infectious diseases and illiteracy declined.

The Italian government after 1900 clearly reflected these developments. Under the guidance of Giovanni Giolitti, the foremost liberal statesman of the era, the state authorities shifted away from the repressive policies of the previous decades and began to seek the support of the parties of the left. In pursuit of this objective, he recognized the legitimacy of labor unions, provided state aid to labor cooperatives, and respected the civil rights of the Socialist party. As conceived by Giolitti, such concessions would reduce mass discontent, isolate violent extremists, and strengthen the position of moderate, reformist elements within the Socialist party. Under the tutelage of the reformists, the party could then be induced to participate as junior partners in an enlarged government coalition under his leadership.

In the short run, Giolitti's strategy seemed to work. The years 1908 to 1910, in particular, represented a golden age for the reformist socialists. They emerged triumphant at the Socialist party congress of 1908. The following year they nearly doubled their parliamentary strength,

Benito, the revolutionary firebrand of Forlì

while their union allies took control of the General Confederation of Labor, a body that represented the chambers of labor and union federations throughout the country. Under the leadership of reformists, the Socialist party adopted a moderate program of demands for universal suffrage, new social welfare legislation, progressive taxation, and education that addressed the aspirations of the country's northern labor aristocracy.

Even as Mussolini took charge of the Forlì Socialists in 1910, however, there were already indications of an explosive discontent within the poorer segments of Italy's work force that belied the complacency of the reformist leadership. Such discontent only grew with the downturn in the Italian economy at the end of the decade. After 1908, industrial growth slowed. The combination of economic recession and an employers' counteroffensive had a devastating impact on employment, wages, and living conditions of Italian workers in the countryside and cities. As a result of these problems and government cutbacks in public works projects, the phenomenon of agricultural unemployment reached alarming new heights, above all in Emilia and Mussolini's home region of Romagna. Not surprisingly, mass unemployment and the refusal of employers to accept collective bargaining enhanced the position of extremist elements within the labor movement.

This situation was tailor-made for a man of Mussolini's temperament and demagogic talents and he quickly took advantage of it. From the outset, he used the pages of his Forlì weekly to launch fierce broadsides against the reformists who controlled the socialist newspaper *Avanti!*, the party's executive committee, and the Socialist Parliamentary Group, whom he accused of having corrupted and compromised the ideals of socialism. The socialist daily had become, in his view, so "bourgeois" that it was little more than "a liberal national organ." Similarly, he blamed the "intoxication" of the party with "electoral-ism" on the influence of reformist lawyers who "like priests, must lie to live." Against these forces, Benito positioned himself as the intransi-gent voice of Romagnole socialism and the pure and dedicated embodiment of "total revolu-tion." In this role, he called for a more passion-ate, violent, and extra-parliamentary movement that would wage a relentless and uncompromis-ing war against the propertied classes.

Significantly, Mussolini backed up his rhetoric with actions. At the reformist-controlled Socialist congress in October 1910, for instance, he achieved a certain notoriety for his scathing speech to a hostile audience, attacking the moder-ate leadership, and for his efforts to get the revo-lutionary faction to secede from the party. When revolutionaries chose to preserve Socialist unity and remain within the party, he took matters into his own hands. In the spring of 1911, he orches-trated the secession of the Forlì Socialists from the national organization. None of these initiatives produced any tangible results, but they did raise Benito's political profile and helped establish him as a rising star on the revolutionary left.

Later, in the early fall of 1911, Mussolini seized another opportunity to gain publicity when Giolitti's government announced plans to expand Italy's colonial holdings by invading the

North African territory of Libya. Not content with his usual editorial attacks on Italian militarism, patriotism, and imperialism, Mussolini promoted a general strike to protest the Libyan War that led to violent demonstrations and acts of sabotage in Forlì. In the immediate aftermath, he took public credit for the sabotage, boasting how "proletarian Forlì" had displayed "a new revolutionary mentality which is . . . smashing to pieces reformist pacifism." A few weeks later, the authorities arrested Mussolini on charges of inciting criminal acts and class hatred. In November 1911 he was convicted and spent the next five months in prison. Arrest and imprisonment, however, only increased his status as a celebrity of sorts within the Italian left.

Developments in the following year, 1912, accelerated Mussolini's astonishingly rapid rise to national prominence. To begin with, the Libyan War had powerful domestic repercussions that worked decisively to Benito's political advantage. From the outset, the war alienated Giolitti from his reformist allies and discredited them and their policies with the rank-and-file of the Socialist party. By the time Mussolini came out of prison in the spring of 1912, the balance of power within the party had shifted dramatically to the revolutionary wing headed by a faction that included his old mentors Giacinto Menotti Serrati and Angelica Balabanoff. With the backing of a solid majority of the delegates, they took control of the national leadership in July at the Socialist party congress in Reggio Emilia. Mussolini's speech to the assembly brilliantly captured the mood of the congress with its eloquent evocation of revolutionary purity, its demagogic attacks on parliament and the monarchy, and its impassioned call for the expulsion of the reformist leaders from the party. The congress agreed with him, expelling a number of reformist deputies and electing a new party directorate that included Balabanoff and Mussolini. More importantly, the young Romagnole Socialist exploited his recent fame, his connections, his proven talents as a journalist, and the paucity of qualified candidates on the extreme left to win an appointment as editor-in-chief of the national party organ, *Avanti!*, in December 1912. In one remarkable year, he had gone from a marginal provincial agitator to the highest ranks of the Italian Socialist party. At the age of 29, Mussolini occupied one of the most important posts in the party and had arrived on the national political scene.

Benito's meteoric rise to prominence on the Italian left imposed important changes in his personal life as well. Late in 1912, he abandoned his home base in Forlì and relocated with Rachele, their baby daughter, Edda, and his mother-in-law to a small apartment in Milan, one of Italy's largest cities, where *Avanti!* was published. The move and his new prominence did not make him any more of a faithful husband than he had been in the past. Despite his family responsibilities, Mussolini embarked on new romantic adventures within months of his arrival in the industrial capital of Italy. The first and most enduring involved the art critic of *Avanti!*, Margherita Sarfatti. Born into an affluent Venetian Jewish family, Sarfatti was a married woman as well as an active socialist and feminist when the two met. She remained Mussolini's mistress and confidante for the next 20 years and, in that capacity, exercised a tremendous influence on him in the arena of the arts and cultural matters. During the same period, Benito also had a more passionate but stormy affair with Leda Rafanelli, an anarchist, convert to Islam, and proponent of free love. To complicate matters further, he also rekindled an old relationship with Ida Dalser, a lover from his days in Trent.

Mussolini's chaotic personal life did not seem to detract from his remarkable success as editor of *Avanti!* Although he had never worked on a national daily newspaper before, he rapidly established himself as one of the foremost Italian journalists of the pre-war era. Upon assuming his office, he purged the paper of its reformist staff members and replaced them with his loyal supporters. To improve the finances of *Avanti!*, increase its prestige, and broaden its base of support, he introduced new technology, eliminated chronic budget deficits, and invited prominent libertarians, revolutionary syndicalists, and southern intellectuals to contribute articles. Mussolini also dramatically changed the style and tone of *Avanti!* Under his tutelage, the paper embraced a belligerent, inflammatory, staccato style and rhetoric on behalf of his vision of the Socialist party as a militant vanguard leading a mass "army" of revolution. As he put it, his goal was to "create inside of the proletariat a strong, aware, daring minority who at the opportune moment can replace the bourgeois minority. The masses will follow and obey them." Predictably, the paper actively encouraged and promoted popular discontent by supporting all strikes and anti-government demonstrations as part of "the psychological preparation of the proletariat for the use of violence."

In the short run, Mussolini's aggressive brand of journalism achieved impressive results. The popularity of *Avanti!* grew by leaps and bounds. By mid-1914, its readership touched the 100,000 mark, roughly four times what it had been when he had taken over the paper a year and a half earlier. Moreover, his propaganda seemed to raise the revolutionary spirit of the rank-and-file. A record number of workers took part in more than 900 strikes in 1913. In the elections of the same year, the Socialist party won a million votes and more than doubled its parliamentary representation, while in 1914 it improved its position in the local elections with Mussolini winning a seat on the Milan municipal council. The mood of popular rebellion reached its peak in early June 1914 when a violent clash between leftist demonstrators and police in the city of Ancona sparked what soon became known as Red Week. A general strike in the Adriatic port city quickly spread to the rest of the country with Mussolini's enthusiastic endorsement and support. When railroad workers joined in the strike, government communications and troop movements broke down, allowing a wave of insurrections to spread over Romagna and the neighboring region of the Marches. It took a week before the various revolts gradually subsided and the government regained control of the situation.

Mussolini exploited his position at the paper and within the leadership of the Socialist party to strengthen his credentials as an intellectual and to bolster his personal standing and authority with the masses. In 1913 he organized a series of public lectures on socialist culture throughout the country and founded his own theoretical journal, *Utopia*, which brought him into contact with a broad range of radical and dissident thinkers. Above all, Mussolini used his new positions to hone his ever more compelling talents as a public speaker. While his speeches created the illusion of spontaneity, he carefully prepared and controlled them with meticulous attention to phrasing, tone, and physical gestures. Commenting on the young firebrand's impact on his audiences, one observer noted how he had "that ascetic presence, that voice like the rustling of leaves in a forest, [which] exercises fatally a hypnotic and captivating power."

By the summer of 1914, Mussolini had established himself as the young star of Italian socialism, albeit more by the force of his charismatic personality than by the coherence of his ideas and political proposals. For a growing segment of the rank-and-file, he had come to embody in his rhetoric and his physical presence the heroic image of the "new socialist man" whose strong, virile, intransigent, and pure character would lead them out of the corruption and compromises of a liberal political system to the promised land. His dynamism and seemingly unwavering devotion to the cause made him an inspirational figure to a younger generation of Socialist militants that included Antonio Gramsci,

Angelo Tasca, and Amadeo Bordiga, the future founders of the Italian Communist party. As Tasca reported approvingly at the time, "almost all the young men are with him and are counting on him to renew the party." The same qualities alarmed his enemies within the party, who warned that he had created a "dictatorship which has an individual basis." His popularity and prominence on the left appeared to receive official validation in the spring of 1914 when delegates to the annual Socialist party congress reconfirmed the leadership of his revolutionary faction.

With all his newfound fame, Mussolini's position in the upper echelons of the party was far from secure and unassailable, however. To begin with, his own bid to win a seat in parliament from Forlì had ended in failure in 1913 when a Republican candidate beat him out. More seriously, the violence he had relentlessly promoted after 1912 failed to achieve any concrete political results by the summer of 1914. On the contrary, it exposed the limitations of his methods of direct action as well as his faction's failure to develop any long-term plan for how to achieve revolution. The outcome of Red Week, in particular, brought out the shortcomings in Mussolini's demagogic tactics. While he enthusiastically encouraged the strikes and riots of that week, the explosion of popular unrest had caught him and his colleagues by surprise and revealed how clueless they were about actually implementing their strategy of revolution. Without central leadership or coordination, the various local insurrections rapidly fizzled out. As a result, the political right emerged as the chief beneficiary of Red Week when Italy's propertied classes rallied behind a more conservative government headed by Antonio Salandra. In the aftermath of the failed revolts, Mussolini came under increasing attack from the moderate wing of the Socialist party, who attempted unsuccessfully to have him removed from the editorship of *Avanti!* Even leaders of his own faction, like Serrati, expressed reservations about his reliance on improvisation and appeals to the "amorphous masses" of the "unorganized." Certainly, the poverty of results raised the prospect that the balance of power within the party might easily shift back in favor of the reformists, ending the young firebrand's brief moment in the sun.

For his part, a disillusioned Mussolini blamed the failures of Red Week on internal divisions within the Socialist party and its resulting reluctance to act decisively in support of the revolts. These criticisms reflected a more general frustration with the structure and organizational methods of the Socialist party. While Mussolini navigated very effectively as a tactician and factional politician, his authoritarian temperament made him increasingly impatient with the realities of the party's democratic procedures. In particular, he bridled at the need for constant negotiations, maneuvers, and compromises that made quick and decisive action virtually impossible. The only solution in his mind entailed the creation of a new type of Socialist party, one that was explicitly revolutionary in orientation, without factions, guided by a concrete program of struggle, and buttressed by an equally unified and focused labor movement.

Mussolini had little time to luxuriate in his successes or worry about his opponents within the Socialist party. International developments in the summer of 1914 quickly overshadowed internal partisan political concerns. On June 28, a team of Serbian assassins killed Archduke Franz Ferdinand, heir to the throne of the Austro-Hungarian Empire, in Sarajevo, Bosnia. When negotiations failed to resolve the ensuing crisis, the Austrians declared war on Serbia on July 28. Within a week this local conflict mushroomed into a general European war as Germany, Russia, France, and England rushed to the aid of their respective allies. The ensuing conflict ushered in a quarter century of catastrophic warfare, revolution, counterrevolution, and economic crises that effectively destroyed Europe's dominant role in the world.

The outbreak of hostilities in August caught the Italian government of Antonio Salandra poised between two opposing alliance systems. Formally tied to Germany and Austria-Hungary in the Triple Alliance, Italy also continued to maintain friendly relations with Great Britain and had limited treaties with France and Russia. A combination of foreign and domestic considerations led the Salandra government to declare Italy's neutrality in August 1914. In part, the government justified its decision, citing the army's lack of preparedness and Austria-Hungary's refusal to provide firm guarantees for Italian territorial compensation. In the wake of Red Week, Salandra also feared that military intervention might provoke renewed domestic disorder that would disrupt any war effort and further undermine internal stability. The decision for neutrality suited the general drift of public opinion in Italy during the summer of 1914. The Socialist party and the trade unions were militantly pacifist, while the Radicals, Republicans, and other democrats opposed intervention in what they viewed as a dynastic war of expansion. Despite their partiality to the Habsburgs, most Catholics also displayed little enthusiasm for war. Only a small group of nationalists and conservatives advocated belligerence in the first weeks of the war, either for reasons of national prestige or out of a sense of loyalty to the Triple Alliance.

This broad national consensus, however, disintegrated in the fall of 1914. With the halt of the German advance in the west and the beginning of an Austrian retreat in the east in September, a movement in favor of Italian intervention on the side of the Entente powers, England, France, and Russia, began to gain momentum within government circles and in the country at large. The ensuing national political debate on the war sharpened divisions within the liberal governing class and shattered the initial unity of the left. While the Socialist party remained firmly committed to absolute neutrality, the democratic left as well as other non-socialist radicals began to advocate participation in a "war of liberation" against autocratic Germany.

The outbreak of World War I confronted Mussolini with one of the most fateful decisions of his political career. At first, he did not appreciate the full significance of the escalating international crisis. In the month after the assassination of Franz Ferdinand, he continued to focus on the domestic repercussions of Red Week. When hostilities erupted in early August 1914, Mussolini toed the party line that called for Italy's absolute neutrality in the conflict. On the eve of war, he penned an article in *Avanti!*, titled

"Down with the War," in which he called on the "Italian proletariat" to abide by the "old password: 'Not one man, not one soldier' at whatever cost!" Indeed, he was one of the most outspoken advocates of extreme measures against the war. Late in July, for instance, he wanted the party to proclaim an insurrectionary general strike in the event that the government decided to join in the impending hostilities.

A number of circumstances, however, led Mussolini to reconsider his initial antiwar stance and question the wisdom of the Socialist party's commitment to absolute neutrality in the first two months of the European conflict. The decision of the socialist parties in France and Germany to support their respective governments' war efforts seemed to make a mockery of the European socialist ideals of working class solidarity, internationalism, and antimilitarism that he had advocated before 1914. Moreover, Mussolini's personal sympathies drew him naturally to the French and British and against the German and Austrian authorities who had treated him so badly during his time as an agitator in Switzerland and Trent. Moreover, many of his non-socialist friends—men like the Florentine intellectual Giuseppe Prezzolini, the southern democrat Gaetano Salvemini, and the syndicalist leader Filippo Corridoni—began to come out in favor of Italian intervention in the conflict. Despite their divergent agendas, all of them saw the war as an extraordinary opportunity to transform what they considered a bankrupt liberal parliamentary system and to modernize Italian society and polity, a vision that appealed strongly to the young socialist leader. Finally, Benito's own impatient and aggressive character made him temperamentally incapable of accepting indefinitely the passive, "cowardly" role of spectator that his party's rigid anti-war stance seemed to impose on him.

After weeks of indecision, Mussolini's growing discontent with a policy he viewed as "suicidal" and his fear that he would be left behind by the most dynamic revolutionary elites, who had already embraced the war, pushed him to make the leap without consulting other members of the party executive. On October 18 he published an editorial in the pages of *Avanti!* attacking absolute neutrality as an "immobilizing" and "backward-looking" position and advocating instead a more active approach to the war. As he told his readers: "We have the privilege of living at the most tragic hour in world history. Do we—as men and as socialists—want to be inert spectators of this huge drama? Or do we want to be . . . the protagonists?" The editorial did not necessarily mean that Mussolini intended to leave the Socialist party. He was initially confident that his popularity with the rank-and-file would enable him to take an independent position on the war and eventually win over the majority of the party to his views.

As he quickly discovered, Mussolini had not only misjudged the situation, but he also had disastrously overestimated both his clout within the party leadership and the depth of his popularity with the socialist masses. The day after his pro-war editorial appeared, he met with the party executive committee in a stormy session. Virtually all of his comrades, including his old mentors Balabanoff and Serrati, voted against his pro-war position. An angry Mussolini demanded an emergency party congress and, when that proposal was also rejected, he resigned his post as editor of *Avanti!* This decision meant that he had relinquished the public platform to defend himself and his pro-war views within the Socialist party. Moreover, his enthusiastic following with the rank-and-file evaporated almost overnight. In their eyes, the former "new socialist man" now became a turncoat, an ambitious and opportunistic politician without firm ideas or principles. When his case came before an assembly of the Milanese branch of the Socialist party in late November 1914, the audience greeted him with shouts of "traitor," "sell-out," and "assassin." His own speech met with the repeated query, "Who is paying you?" (Chi paga?) Predictably, the assembly voted overwhelmingly his expulsion from the party, and the image of the opportunist and turncoat did not dissipate with time. In fact, it would color all subsequent portraits of Mussolini by his former comrades within the socialist and organized labor movements.

While Benito insisted that he still remained a socialist and a revolutionary, the accusations of his former followers seemed to have had some justification. After October 18 he displayed no qualms about aligning himself with powerful economic interests whom he had been violently denouncing as capitalist oppressors of the proletariat for over a decade. Less than a month after his resignation from *Avanti!*, he reemerged as the editor and owner of a new pro-war daily, *Il Popolo d'Italia*. Significantly, the money to launch the paper came from wealthy landowning circles in Bologna and a group of industrialists who stood to profit from Italian intervention in the war. His decision to accept such patronage as well as subsidies from the French secret service in order to launch a daily in direct opposition to the official organ of the Socialist party had profound consequences. Above all, it meant that he had burned his bridges to the political community that had been his natural home for the previous 12 years.

Mussolini's decision to abandon the Socialist party and link up with conservative forces does not appear to have simply been the product of greed or personal ambition. The accusation that he had sold out for money is not credible, since Mussolini never displayed much interest in amassing great wealth or indulging in personal luxuries. Nor did his adoption of a pro-war stance promise to enhance immediately his own power and influence. On the contrary, he had sacrificed a prominent role in an established national party in order to pursue a precarious new political course whose direction and outcome were very uncertain in the winter of 1914–1915. At the same time, his decision to break with the socialist movement did not grow out of a coherent, long-term political strategy. Before 1914, Mussolini had voiced frustration with party doctrines that limited his freedom of action. He also had displayed, on occasion, a certain appreciation for the ideas of non-socialist writers and for the achievements of the more modern sectors of Italian industry. But these tendencies attested more to his intellectual eclecticism than to his clarity as a strategic thinker.

Instead the dramatic reversals of the fall of 1914 resulted from a combination of impulsiveness, miscalculation, improvisation, and short-term political considerations on Mussolini's part. His aggressive personality and thirst for action for action's sake clashed with the official pacifism of the socialists. Increasingly impatient with party orthodoxy and misjudging the mood of his comrades, he took the fateful step of publicly endorsing Italian intervention. His sudden change of opinion about the war then set in motion a chain of events that he no longer controlled. Confronted with an unanticipated rejection by his comrades, he responded with a series of improvised actions, such as the launching of a new paper, that expressed not so much a long-term political vision as a desperate attempt to reestablish himself as a major figure on the national scene. After he had burned his bridges with the socialist movement, his own political survival required him to find new friends and media outlets elsewhere. He had little choice but to try to find them in the ranks of pro-war industrialists, nationalists, and right-wing interventionists.

Significantly, Mussolini's political views began to evolve in accordance with his rapidly shifting sets of friends and enemies. Although he still claimed to speak for a pro-war socialism and employed his old revolutionary rhetoric after November 1914, the substance and meaning of his revolution began to change in fundamental respects. To begin with, his new vision no longer focused on the cause of the working class or socialist internationalism as it had in the past. In the pages of *Il Popolo d'Italia*, class and class conflict ceased to be the great agencies of historical change. Now he wrote instead of the "producers"—the supposedly best and brightest from all segments of Italian society who must collaborate on behalf of the "nation." In place of the old idea of social revolution, he advanced the notion of a "revolutionary war," a war not to overthrow the bourgeois order and build a socialist paradise, but rather to create a new, more efficient, but essentially capitalist society. Likewise, the onetime fiery anti-monarchist and anti-militarist was urging a "sacred union" with the monarchy and the conservative Salandra government in the spring of 1915 to ensure intervention and ultimate victory on the battlefront. The violent enemy of Giolitti's imperialist war in Libya in 1911 now advocated Italian territorial expansion into the Alps and the Balkans.

Although Mussolini's ideas and allegiances began to change, the political style, rhetoric, and methods that characterized his years as a revolutionary socialist remained the same. His glorification of violence and direct action as well as his predilection for inflammatory slogans and verbal assaults on his enemies continued to inform his journalism and politics. Only now they were directed against the Socialist party and other parliamentary and Catholic exponents of Italian neutrality rather than the monarchy or conservative propertied classes. Thus, he denounced socialists variously as the "worst sort of cowards," "hysterics," and "cannibals." Parliament was, in his words, "the pestiferous pustule poisoning the blood of the nation. It must be wiped out." In the case of the socialists, his violence was more than rhetorical. In the early months of 1915, he fought a series of duels with former party comrades. At the same time, Mussolini also moved to organize politically the ranks of the interventionist left. In December he took charge of the *Fasci di Azione Rivoluzionario*, or revolutionary action groups, which he promoted as "a free association of subversives from all schools and political points of view." Under his leadership, the *Fasci* embarked upon a campaign of propaganda, demonstrations, and violence in support of Italian intervention in the war in the spring of 1915.

Benito's break with the socialist movement also altered the contours of his perennially complicated love life. Angelica Balabanoff and Leda Rafanelli, two women with whom he had been intimate before 1914, immediately severed all ties with him after his conversion to the interventionist cause. Balabanoff, in particular, developed a personal hatred of her former protege and lover, voting against him in the Socialist party executive and later writing accounts that depicted him as a neurotic and a coward. His mistress on the staff of *Avanti!*, Margherita Sarfatti, chose instead to stand by her man, following him out of the Socialist party and into the ranks of the interventionist left. He found additional solace in the arms of another old lover, Ida Dalser. Their liaison resulted in a child, Benito Albino, who was born in November 1915; Mussolini recognized the child and paid his mother alimony and child support, though he did not see the boy. These developments did not keep Benito from cementing his ties with his common-law wife, Rachele. He officially tied the knot with Rachele in December 1915, and the two celebrated the birth of their first son, Vittorio, in September of the following year.

In the short run, Mussolini appeared to have backed a winning cause, even if the heterogeneous pro-war coalition of conservatives, nationalists, democrats, and dissident socialists represented only a small minority of the Italian public. Their strategic influence in the media and other centers of power enabled them to seize the initiative from the less organized and politically fragmented neutralist majority. More importantly, the Salandra government and monarchy secretly negotiated with the French, English, and Russians the Treaty of London, which was signed in late April, committing Italy to enter the war within one month in exchange for guarantees that Italy would receive the Trentino, the South Tyrol, Istria, the city of Trieste and a few Dalmatian Islands after the defeat of Germany and Austria. Meanwhile, a noisy interventionist campaign in the press and the streets of the major cities created the illusion of popular support for war in the spring of 1915. The pro-war campaign culminated in the "radiant days of May" and Italy's entrance into World War I.

The triumph of the interventionist movement, however, did little to improve Mussolini's own political fortunes. On the contrary, Italy's entry into the war left him isolated and at the margins of national public life. As became quickly apparent, Benito's break with the socialists over the issue of war had deprived him of his old familiar community and the comradeship that had sustained him throughout his life, without providing him a comparable political base elsewhere. After October 1914, he found few converts to the interventionist cause within the ranks of the socialist movement or, as he put it, among "the young of Italy, . . . the young of that generation which fate has driven to make history." His efforts to appeal to new constituencies of non-socialist radicals, democratic idealists, patriots, and even imperialists met with equally scant success. His paper, *Il Popolo d'Italia,* had a mere 1,600 subscribers in the spring of 1915, while the *Fasci d'azione rivo-luzionari*, at their peak, claimed no more than 5,000 members. Nor did his oratorical skills bring him the accustomed attention and adoration of the interventionist rank-and-file. Even at the peak of the pro-war demonstrations in May, Benito was second to more famous and eloquent public speakers like the legendary poet and bon vivant Gabriele D'Annunzio. At the same time, Mussolini did not find a secure political home among his collaborators on the right. His wealthy conservative patrons, for instance, were content to exploit his demagogic services during the interventionist campaign, but once Italy entered the war they had little use for him or his paper. The right-wing Nationalist Association, for its part, refused to accept the former revolutionary socialist as anything more than an undesirable ally. To make matters worse, Benito's modest family and social background, always an asset within the socialist community, became a liability in the affluent interventionist camp, where he came across as a provincial redneck among the more educated, sophisticated, and refined luminaries of the propertied classes. By the fall of 1915, it seemed that the overly ambitious young man from Predappio had had his proverbial fifteen minutes of fame and now was condemned to a future of anonymous obscurity.

However, Mussolini had little time to lament his choices or prospects. In September 1915, he was drafted into the army. By then, the Italian front with Austria had already settled into the static slaughter that characterized the western front after the first two Battles of Isonzo that resulted in more than 100,000 casualties. He spent the next year and a half as a regular infantryman in the trenches high in the Alps. While the absence of any major battles gave him little opportunity for heroism, he was evidently popular with his fellow soldiers and enjoyed the respect of his superiors, who promoted him to the rank of corporal. Benito's war ended abruptly in February 1917, when he was wounded by shrapnel in a training accident. After a period of recuperation in a military hospital, he received an honorable discharge from the army and returned to civilian life in the summer of 1917.

Mussolini spent the remainder of the war years on the home front in a desperate search for an ideological formula or a political stance that might bring him public notoriety and permit him to reemerge as an important and influential figure on the national scene. As in the past, he relied on his journalist's skills to pursue his goals. He immediately set out to revive the fortunes of *Il Popolo d'Italia*, which had fallen on hard times during his stint in the military. Under his renewed tutelage, the paper advanced a rather contradictory agenda that combined demagogic appeals to the masses with nationalistic demands for territorial annexation and ultra-patriotic attacks on the Socialist party and other supposed "defeatists." Especially after the disastrous defeat of the Italian army at the Battle of Caporetto in late 1917 and the Austrian occupation of the northeastern corner of the country, Mussolini demanded authoritarian measures to discipline all segments of society on behalf of the war effort. Accordingly, he called for the suppression of the Socialist party press, the dismantling of parliament, and the creation of a military dictatorship, on the grounds that "a few thousands" could not be allowed the "freedom to betray their country," while "millions of men" were off fighting for the nation.

In the wake of Caporetto, Mussolini continued during the last year of the war to distance himself from his revolutionary socialist past and to advance views more in accord with the interests of the war industries whose subsidies sustained the paper. He now began to dismiss Marxism as a "heap of ruins," while denouncing the leader of the world's first communist revolution in Russia, Vladimir Lenin, as a traitor working for the Germans. Similarly, the masthead of *Il Popolo d'Italia* now announced that the daily was the voice of the "soldiers and producers" rather than a "Socialist Newspaper" as in the past. In its pages, Benito advanced his vision of the future, one that had little to do with socialism. To begin with, he envisioned a government led by the "trenchocracy," a new elite of warriors, whose shared experiences in the front lines of the war gave them the strength and moral credibility to guide the country in the post-war era. This new elite rested, in turn, on an alliance of bourgeois and proletarian "producers" that would eliminate the "parasites" and maximize production on behalf of the Italian nation.

The sudden end of hostilities on the western front in November 1918 brought to a close Mussolini's wartime press campaigns and ushered in a new era of uncertainty for the thirty-five-year-old ex-socialist journalist. Although he greeted the victory of the Entente with predicable enthusiasm, he must have recognized that the return to peacetime deprived him of the issues that had principally defined his public identity and activity since the fall of 1914. Of course, he still enjoyed a certain fame among avant-garde intellectuals and revolutionary interventionists at the end of the war, but these small groups hardly constituted the basis for a significant mass movement. In the absence of war, he had no clear role to play or constituency to mobilize and lead into the political fray. At the same time, however, the period of instability, popular discontent, and bitter social conflict that came with the return of peacetime conditions also created extraordinary opportunities for a man of Mussolini's talents as a demagogic orator, instinctive politician, and ruthless opportunist.

III

Mussolini and the Fascist Rise to Power

1919–1924

The end of World War I did not bring any quick return to the "good old days" of the prewar era. On the contrary, the cease-fire in late 1918 ushered in one of the most tumultuous periods in modern European history. While revolutions swept away the old empires of Central and Eastern Europe, the victorious powers in the west faced unparalleled social conflict and political unrest. The sudden return to peace had immediate domestic repercussions in Italy, for in no other victorious country were public expectations of sweeping change so pronounced and widespread. In the spring of 1919, the leading Italian daily, *Il Corriere della Sera*, captured the mood of euphoria that characterized society in the first months of peace:

The end of the war has removed that moral force which constrained every citizen to control himself, to wait with patience, to limit his own desires. Now that this bridle has broken, all aspirations have a free field and all desires have been unchained. Everyone seems to feel the need to live newly his life. It is no longer the old life, which today appears so serene and easy, but a new life that must be full, rich, more than before.

Italians from every walk of life came to see broad political and social change as an inevitable feature of the world emerging from the war. Demands for constitutional reform, land to the peasants, workers' control of the factories, and governmental regulation of industry now dominated all political discussions.

The economic realities of postwar Italy, however, precluded even the partial satisfaction of popular expectations. The war had taken a heavy toll on the economy: The pattern of industry had been distorted, the land exhausted, the balance of trade disrupted, and the railroad system allowed to deteriorate seriously. With the return of peace, the war industries cut back on their production and laid off thousands of workers, precisely at a time when soldiers were flooding back into the labor market. Unemployment, which had virtually disappeared during the war, reached alarming levels in the spring of 1919.

Skyrocketing inflation compounded the plight of unemployed workers and veterans. The termination of wartime allied supports had a disastrous impact on the Italian monetary system. By mid-1919 the general price index had quadrupled its prewar levels and showed no signs of leveling off.

Diplomatic setbacks at the Paris Peace Conference in 1919 further inflamed domestic discontent. The Italian delegation went to Paris to achieve a "victorious peace" based on the Treaty of London of 1915, which promised Italy sizable border territories with large Slavic and German-speaking populations as well as colonial compensation in the event of a victory by the Entente powers. By 1919, however, the powerful presence of the United States and its president, Woodrow Wilson, at the peace table confronted the Italian government with a set of unanticipated challenges. The Americans had never signed the Treaty of London and felt no obligation to honor its terms. Wilson argued instead that the frontiers of Italy should be adjusted along clear lines of nationality. Wilsonian resistance to their claims finally led the Italian delegation to walk out of the conference in protest and return home early in April 1919. While this gesture aroused an enormous patriotic fervor in the public at home, it had little effect on the peace conference, where the United States, Great

Britain, and France carried on without Italy in arranging the postwar territorial settlement. After a month, the prospect of further isolation and the loss of both reparations from Germany and supplies from the victorious powers forced Italy to back down. In early May, the humiliated Italian delegation returned to the Paris conference. As a consequence, the government failed to win any concessions at the peace table and aroused the wrath of nationalists within Italy, who attacked it for having "mutilated" Italy's military victory in 1918.

Such foreign policy failures and dire economic conditions had immediate social consequences. High unemployment and inflation triggered not only an extraordinary resurgence of strikes and labor demonstrations, but also more chaotic and explosive forms of social protest. During the summer of 1919, Italy became the scene of a wave of "cost of living" riots in virtually all of the major cities. Meanwhile in the south, peasant war veterans began to act unilaterally on the government's wartime promises of land by seizing tens of thousands of acres without prior consent of the owners. The Nationalists and various paramilitary groups added to the confusion with violent counterdemonstrations and an aggressive campaign for the territories that had been promised to Italy in 1915.

Italy's old governing class was unprepared to cope with the breakdown of old loyalties and respect for law and order in the first year of peace. Bitter divisions over the war, foreign policy, and domestic reform accentuated the preexisting fragmentation of the liberals. As a result, the postwar governments lacked the parliamentary political support needed to deal effectively with mass unrest and right-wing sedition. Throughout much of 1919, political leaders in Rome ricocheted from one emergency to another with improvised measures that alienated both the right and the left. In the absence of strong guidance from Rome, the public administration of law and order gradually broke down into a myriad of isolated state officials at the provincial level, each increasingly susceptible to pressures from the most aggressive local forces.

Although these conditions seemed to be tailor-made for a man of Mussolini's demagogic talents as a journalist and rabble-rouser, the ex-socialist and radical interventionist struggled throughout 1919 to find the right formula for political success. As he later conceded, the end of the war left him "lost and searching for a road." Initially, he adopted a political strategy that mixed radicalism and superpatriotism to appeal to industrial workers and peasants as well as returning war veterans. On March 23, 1919, Mussolini joined with a few hundred Futurist intellectuals, nationalists, anarchists, and *arditi*, men from the elite fighting unit of the Italian army, in Milan to found a new political movement, the *Fascio di Combattimento* or Fighting Group. The program adopted by these "Fascists of the first hour" sought to attract followers from both the left and the right. Thus, they advocated universal suffrage, an end to the monarchy, an eight-hour day for workers, land to the peasants, and a special high tax rate on war profits. At the same time, they espoused a violent anti-socialism, glorified the Great War, and demanded an expansionist foreign policy with Italian annexation of border territories in the former Austro-Hungarian Empire.

This *Fascio*, the kernel of the original Fascist movement, was distinguished less by its ideological coherence than by its political style and methods. Mussolini designed the movement to express and embody not a precise political project so much as a state of mind, a pervasive mood of postwar discontent and undirected revolt. In a conscious effort to separate the fledgling group from the established political parties, he proclaimed that the *Fascio* rejected all "credos" and "dogmas." On other occasions, he portrayed Fascism as an "anti-party" and a "church of all heresies," whose members enjoyed "the luxury of being both aristocrats and democrats." All of these slogans sought to project the image of a new type of movement with a highly flexible structure devoid of rigid rules and regulations and tailored to a population fed up with wartime bureaucracies and restrictions. Such flexibility offered additional benefits to Mussolini, since it allowed him to adapt his tactics to attract new members and to pursue alliances across the normal divisions between right and left. Not surprisingly, the Fascists' initial recruits included left-wing interventionists, veterans, right-wing nationalists, reactionaries, and street fighters.

Above all, the early Fascists promised violent action rather than talk. As Mussolini put it, Fascism stood out as "an organization not for propaganda but for battle." Already in the winter of 1918–1919, he began to use combat-hardened ex-*arditi* as personal bodyguards at *Il Popolo d'Italia*. Moreover, less than a month after the founding meeting of the *Fascio di Combattimento*, an armed contingent of *arditi* and Futurists attacked and destroyed the headquarters of the Socialist party daily, *Avanti!*, on April 15, 1919. While he played no part in this first "punitive expedition"—the term that the Fascists applied to their violent assaults—Mussolini quickly saw its potential for attracting attention and mobilizing supporters, and he immediately stepped forward to claim "full moral responsibility for the episode." In the aftermath, he accentuated the paramilitary character of the Fascist movement by promoting the creation of squads of "tried and well-armed individuals" that incorporated the black-shirted uniforms and the martial rituals and values of the *arditi*. These squads existed to attack any and all enemies of Fascism.

Despite the notoriety he attracted after the attack of the Socialist paper, Mussolini's initial foray into the turbulent world of postwar Italian politics met with surprisingly little success in 1919. Indeed, events in the second half of the year dramatically demonstrated his utter failure to win a following either among the veterans or among the laboring classes. Within the nationalist camp, Gabriele D'Annunzio, a war hero and Italy's foremost living playwright and poet, completely upstaged Mussolini with a daring action on the country's borders with Yugoslavia. During the summer of 1919, collaboration between the Italian nationalist elements and military officials in the disputed cities of Trieste and Fiume gave rise to rumors of a possible coup d'état. Nationalist activities in the area culminated in September. That month the local garrison in Fiume mutinied and, under the command of D'Annunzio, seized control of that city, in open defiance of the government and the international authorities. D'Annunzio's Fiume Expedition aroused enormous patriotic enthusiasm. Many nationalists abandoned the Fascist movement to join him in the occupied city. For his part, Mussolini could only watch from the sidelines as his more glamorous rival grabbed the public's attention and became the charismatic leader of Italy's national-revolutionary forces.

Mussolini suffered an even more devastating setback in the parliamentary elections of November 1919. Both the timing and the format of the elections, the first under universal manhood suffrage and proportional representation, strongly favored the large, well-organized mass parties. In the year after the war, the Socialist party expanded rapidly and the new Catholic party, the Popular party, enjoyed significant support in the countryside. The Fascist movement, on the other hand, made little organizational headway in the months after its founding. Although a number of new *fasci* emerged in various Italian cities during the spring and summer of 1919, most of them led an ephemeral existence with few members and little or no activity, especially after D'Annunzio's Fiume Expedition. As a result, Mussolini pursued electoral alliances wherever he could find them. His efforts to forge a coalition of pro-war leftists and veterans' groups collapsed, however, when the other parties insisted on his exclusion from the list of candidates on the grounds that his polarizing presence would alienate working-class voters and mean the kiss of death for their electoral slate. Mussolini and the Milanese Fascists had little choice but to campaign in isolation. Elsewhere the local *fasci* tended to join right-wing antigovernment coalitions.

The outcome of the elections of November 16, 1919, ended the parliamentary dominance of Italy's old political class. It also seemed to demonstrate the utter bankruptcy of Mussolini's strategy of blending left-wing and ultrapatriotic appeals. The Socialists, who had run on an explicitly antiwar platform, emerged as the largest single party in the Chamber of Deputies, the elected lower house of the Italian parliament. For their part, the Fascists won only one parliamentary seat in all of Italy. Despite their notoriety, Mussolini and his Milanese *fascio* were shut out completely. They managed to win a mere 4,657 votes out of the 270,000 cast locally. The triumphant Socialists, eager to gloat over their success, paraded in front of their former leader's home with a coffin that symbolically contained the lifeless body of Mussolini's political career. *Avanti!* echoed the theme with a sarcastic news item in which it reported: "A corpse in a state of decomposition was fished out of the canal yesterday. It appears to be that of Mussolini." On the following day, the police raided the offices of Mussolini's paper and briefly jailed him on weapons charges. The Fascist movement appeared to be lifeless in the winter of 1919–1920. Fewer than 4,000 members remained in the entire country, and the revenues of *Il Popolo d'Italia* plummeted. Remarkably, Mussolini managed to maintain an optimistic public front even in the face of these humiliating experiences. A few months after the elections, he confidently predicted how the very success of his adversaries would expose and accentuate their weaknesses and contradictions: "The marvelous victory at the polls has simply shown up the inefficiency and weakness of the socialists. They are impotent alike as reformers and revolutionaries. They take no action either in parliament or in the streets . . . neither reform nor revolution. . . ."

Developments the following year demonstrated the accuracy of Mussolini's analysis. During the first nine months of 1920, bitter political divisions paralyzed the Chamber of Deputies and soaring inflation plagued the economy. The government's authority seemingly collapsed in the face of one of Italy's most prolonged and intense periods of social upheaval. A record number of industrial, agricultural, and public service workers engaged in more than 2,000 strikes and often violent political demonstrations. As the strikes gained momentum, a massive influx of new recruits poured into the socialist unions. Industrialists and landowners voiced alarm not only at the size and violence of the strikes, but also at the radical demands of the strikers. The maximalist leadership of the Socialist party did little to calm the enormous expectations of their followers or the exaggerated fears of the propertied classes. Hailing the strikes as manifestations of revolutionary spirit, the maximalists exhorted the workers to continue using force "to conquer power and consolidate revolutionary conquests."

Such rhetoric, however, masked the weakness of the Socialist party's strategy. Although technically the workers had emerged victorious from the strikes of 1920, their actual conquests fell far short of the sweeping social revolution the Socialist party had led them to expect. With few visible changes in the patterns of daily work, disillusionment replaced enthusiasm and militancy. The onset of a recession in the late fall of 1920, with its accompanying layoffs and weakened bargaining power for the unions, further demoralized workers. The inconclusive outcome of the strikes also sharpened long-standing ideological conflicts within the Socialist party among reformists, maximalists, and communists. These internal conflicts culminated in January 1921 when the extreme left withdrew to form the Communist party of Italy.

In the summer of 1920, political momentum began to shift from the left to the right. Under the leadership of the great pre-war prime minister Giovanni Giolitti, a new government began to address the propertied classes' concerns with social unrest by taking a stronger stand on strikes and leftist violence. Signs of a conservative revival came in the fall with the emergence of cohesive and militant organizations of industrialists and landowners to combat the labor movement. Municipal elections during the same period indicated a similar trend as the antisocialist forces recaptured most of the major cities from the political left. To a certain extent, developments on the Italian peninsula reflected a more general receding of the revolutionary tide throughout Europe after the defeat of the Soviet army outside Warsaw. Not only in Italy, but also in France and Germany, new possibilities appeared for revived conservative leadership based on a coalition of wealthy elites and the middle classes. Yet in the case of Italy, the shift in political momentum from left to right in the fall of 1920 either went unrecognized or came too late to restore the confidence of large segments of the wealthy propertied classes in the country's liberal parliamentary institutions. Instead, they and the middle classes thirsted only for revenge against the socialist forces who, in their view, had humiliated them and violated their property rights. Accordingly, ordinarily respectable and law-abiding men of property now became increasingly prepared to support coercive alternatives to the legal authorities.

The new willingness of Italy's social and economic elites to experiment with violent and extralegal remedies for the ills of the "red tyranny" of the left gave the Fascist movement a renewed lease on life, this time as the vanguard of a patriotic and class reaction against Socialism in the second half of 1920. Already in April of that year, the local leader of the *fascio* in Bologna noted that the sudden enthusiasm of rich landowners and businessmen for vigilante activities was bringing them "into our field of action." Of course, such an alliance between the Fascists and conservative groups required fundamental changes in the structure and function of the movement at the local level. In the course of 1920, the *fasci* in the countryside of Emilia deemphasized the radicalism, national concerns, and informal comraderie of the "Fascists of the first hour." Instead they placed a new stress on the defense of property, expanded recruitment, a more disciplined organization, and above all the training of paramilitary squads to combat the Socialist movement. By the winter of 1920–1921, increasingly militarized provincial Fascist groups in Bologna and Ferrara were ready to launch a series of punitive expeditions against Socialist unions, cooperatives, and political operations. These initial violent forays met with the support of local authorities and elites. In the wake of successes in Bologna and Ferrara, the movement of provincial fascism, with its military organization, armed squads, and punitive expeditions, spread rapidly to other zones of northern and central Italy. Within the span of a few months, this "chaotic ensemble of local reactions" propelled fascism and a surprised Mussolini to sudden political prominence on the national level. He quickly exploited the situation in the provinces by joining a coalition of liberals and nationalists for the parliamentary elections of May 1921. His decision paid off when voters elected Mussolini and a bloc of 35 Fascists to the Chamber of Deputies.

Mussolini played a marginal role in the remarkable expansion of the Fascist movement, which took place largely as a product of local issues and initiatives. As a result, most of the new recruits and sympathizers to the cause initially did not look to Milan for inspiration or guidance. They tended instead to identify with their own provincial Fascist leaders or *ras*, who ruled through a blend of personal charisma, fear, and intimidation. Moreover, these *ras* enjoyed financial independence from Mussolini and the national leadership, since wealthy local patrons financed all of their activities. Likewise, Benito did not have an especially creative role in the development of what became Fascism's most characteristic gestures, customs, and symbols. The Roman salute, the black shirt uniforms, the party anthem, *Giovinezza*, the use of castor oil on adversaries, and ceremonies honoring the fallen all grew out of initiatives at the provincial level or were copied from other political groups.

Nonetheless, Mussolini emerged by the end of 1921 as the dominant figure in the consolidation of Fascism and as a major force on the national political scene because his ideological flexibility, political ambiguity, and tactical opportunism became invaluable assets in the aftermath of the violent offensive against socialism. From the outset, Mussolini benefited from his status as the only national exponent of fascism capable of holding together what was otherwise an uncoordinated and heterogeneous movement of provincial warlords and parochial revolts. The rapid expansion of fascism in the first half of 1921 provoked serious internal tensions and conflicts. By the summer, acute contemporary observers began to speak of two distinct and conflicting fascisms: one associated with the urban nuclei and composed chiefly of veterans, students, and middle-class followers, the other associated with the more rural *fasci* of landowners and peasant farmers.

While the two fascisms shared an aggressive anti-socialism, their motives and objectives often diverged. For many urban Fascists, violence against the socialist movement was linked to an intense patriotism and an idealistic rebellion against all authority. They saw the growing involvement of the rural elites, with their crude antiunion objectives, as a corruption and betrayal of fascism's mission of national redemption. For their part, wealthy converts and supporters in the countryside viewed the movement as an instrument to restore social order and discipline and looked upon the Fascists of the first hour as irresponsible radicals or vulgar thugs. Additional divisions between political and military factions further complicated the internal life of the movement. In this context, Mussolini could adapt his tactics and message to very different local conditions and thereby persuade all factions that somehow he spoke for them and was working on their behalf. To a large extent, the uneasy unity of the movement depended on his ability to appear both as a radical antiestablishment figure and as an ally of the rich and powerful.

Mussolini discovered the difficulties of maintaining this balancing act in the summer of 1921 when he confronted what would be the most serious

internal crisis in fascism's early history. While
the violent actions of the paramilitary squads
had contributed enormously to the popularity
and power of the movement, they had also created new problems for the continued advance of
fascism as a national political force. If Mussolini
treated violence as a means to achieve precise
political objectives, for the *squadristi*, the members of the punitive squads, it was an end in itself, the reason for their collective existence and
the main source of their group spirit. After the
electoral success of May, the relative autonomy
and chaotic violence of the provincial *fasci* not
only reduced Mussolini's margins for parliamentary maneuver in Rome, but also undermined his
personal authority within the movement.

In order to consolidate the political gains of
the previous half year and to impose his control
over the local *ras*, Mussolini launched a proposal
for a "pact of pacification" with the Socialist
party in June 1921. By the first week of August,
both sides had signed an agreement to end violence immediately and to respect each other's organizations. Efforts to impose the pact on his
own movement, however, triggered a sweeping
revolt by a majority of the paramilitary squads
and the provincial Fascist leaders. In mid-August,
representatives of some six hundred *fasci* publicly repudiated the truce with the Socialist party.

Capturing the mood of the revolt, one of its leaders, Dino Grandi, expressed "devotion and affection" for Mussolini but denied him "the exclusive right to do as he wishes with this movement of *ours*, as if he had the authority of a master and an ancient Roman *paterfamilias*."

When talks failed to bring his provincial adversaries into line, Mussolini turned to a divide-and-conquer strategy that succeeded brilliantly in ending the crisis and strengthening his personal power. At the national congress of *fasci* in November in Rome, he split the provincial warlords and won over a majority of delegates by agreeing to abandon the pact of pacification. In exchange for this concession, he gained invaluable support for his proposal to transform the fragmented movement into a disciplined national political party with a formal program and defined hierarchical structure. This solution, however, did not put an end to internal conflicts between the political and military wings of fascism, which would continue intermittently into the mid-1920s, nor did it establish Mussolini as the absolute and unquestioned leader, since he still had to consult with the other members of the party's central committee. Nonetheless, he had won recognition from the provincial bosses as the "Duce," or top man of the new National Fascist party, and in that capacity he was now able to defeat any serious internal challengers. Moreover, as the Duce he benefited from the first constitution of the party, which called for a greater concentration of authority at the center and explicitly emphasized the values of "order, discipline, and hierarchy." Institutionalization of fascism also permitted him to assemble a team of reliable and compliant lieutenants who filled the principal administrative positions of the party. Similarly, he tied the paramilitary squads to local branches of the new party and made them subject to periodic review by national inspectors in order to strengthen his control over the provincial Fascists.

Once he had overcome the first great internal crisis of fascism, Mussolini devoted the next eleven months to the larger task of winning political power at the national level. The conditions that made this goal possible lay in the public's diminishing confidence in Italy's governing class in 1922, the growing breakdown of public order, and the reluctance of either the Socialist or the Catholic parties to take the initiative. Internal divisions within and among the three major political forces in the country weakened all of them and prevented them from forming a strong front against fascism. Governmental weakness in Rome, in turn, fueled escalating political violence by the Black Shirts in the provinces, which further undermined the already diminished prestige of parliamentary institutions. As a result, the Fascists had largely supplanted the state as the effective rulers in a large part of Italy by the middle of the summer.

The breakdown of the liberal state opened up possibilities for the entrance of fascism into the Italian government, and Mussolini's tactical brilliance and ruthless opportunism transformed these opportunities into realities in the fall of 1922. The stunning accession of the Fascists to power in late October was, above all, a personal triumph for the Duce. The key to victory lay in Mussolini's skill in executing a dual strategy that combined legal political maneuvers with preparations for a violent seizure of power. On the one hand, he employed a strident, revolutionary language to stoke the enthusiasm of the Fascist rank-and-file, encouraging them to mobilize for a "march on Rome to force the government to resign, and induce the Crown to form a Fascist cabinet." In a series of speeches in September and early October, for instance, he proclaimed that "there are two governments in Italy today—one too many" and assured the squads that they had begun "the march that can end only when we have reached our final goal, Rome." The party faithfully responded with rallies and demonstrations involving tens of thousands of armed Black Shirts that served as dry runs for an anticipated insurrection. In a similar vein, Mussolini held a meeting in Milan in mid-October to draw up a military plan of action.

At the same time, the Duce of fascism presented himself to Italy's old political and business leaders as a reasonable person open to compromise. To reinforce the sympathy his party already enjoyed in conservative military, business, and governmental circles, Mussolini shifted further to the right in the course of 1922. The new emphasis he put on the virtues of order, discipline, and hierarchy aimed not only to strengthen his control of the party but also to reassure those groups who were uneasy about the illegal and excessive violence of the Fascist squads. The same considerations led him quietly to jettison most of the radical tax and labor proposals of the early Fascist movement. In their place appeared slogans that stressed free enterprise and a "technocratic" modernization of the economy, which appealed to Italian industrialists. Further, to placate the Catholic authorities concerned about his anti-clerical past, he began to speak positively about the church's role and to make direct overtures to the new pope, Pius XI.

Above all, Mussolini's genius lay in his ability to use the threat of a violent seizure of power both to maintain the allegiance of his belligerent supporters and to facilitate legal parliamentary bargaining with other political forces. Throughout October Mussolini skillfully exploited rivalries among the leading Liberal statesmen through separate negotiations to increase the political price for his party's collaboration and support. By the end of the month, they seemed to prefer the idea of the young Fascist leader as prime minister rather than one of their own internal party rivals. On October 28, the provincial warlords began to mobilize their troops with their leader's tacit approval, forcing a confrontation with state authorities in what came to be known as the March on Rome. With armed Fascist squads moving toward the capital, King Victor Emanuel III and his army chiefs faced the difficult choice of declaring martial law with all its accompanying risks of civil war or following legal formalities by inviting the head of the Fascist party to form a new coalition government. The cautious king chose the path of least resistance. Early on October 29, 1922, Victor Emanuel telephoned Milan and offered the top governmental post to the Duce. Two days later, Mussolini arrived in Rome where his supporters organized a victory parade and he took the oath as Italy's youngest prime minister at the age of 39.

While Fascist propagandists would subsequently immortalize the March on Rome as a great revolutionary moment, the triumph of fascism and the consolidation of Mussolini's personal power took considerably more time to accomplish. Unlike his German counterpart, Adolf Hitler, who forged his dictatorship within months of taking office, the Duce would require an additional six years to complete his seizure of power in Italy. Most contemporaries in the fall of 1922 did not see the events of October as marking such a major break with the past. True, Mussolini was a new political leader, representing a new political party, but his path to the head of the government still conformed technically to established parliamentary procedures. Moreover, the political composition of his cabinet looked similar to previous coalition governments and, like them, its survival required a majority in the Chamber of Deputies. While Mussolini occupied the key offices of prime minister or head of government, minister of foreign affairs, and minister of interior, which controlled the police forces, none of the top Fascist warlords received cabinet posts in the new government. Instead, his cabinet included two military officers, one Nationalist, two conservative Catholics, one Liberal, three Democrats, and the philosopher Giovanni Gentile.

The heterogeneous and conservative character of Mussolini's first government reflected, in turn, the limits of his power and freedom of action.

After the March on Rome, he continued to face parliamentary opposition as well as a nominally free press and judiciary. Furthermore, his government rested upon a tiny group of Fascist deputies. Thus, he depended upon a series of compromises with the king and the old Liberal political leaders, who still enjoyed large support in parliament and viewed him as little more than a lesser evil. These establishment allies expected him to restore law and order, and assumed that they could tame him and bring him into the constitutional fold. To make matters worse, Mussolini also had to contend with the anger and frustration of hard-liners within his own party who had expected the March on Rome to make a radical break with the past and impose an all-Fascist government on the country. Not surprisingly, these provincial warlords opposed any return to business as usual and called instead for a "second wave" of violence to sweep away the old parliamentary political order and forge a new and purer Fascist regime.

In the face of these contradictory pressures, Mussolini had little choice but to continue after October 1922 the delicate balancing act that had brought him to Rome, especially since he still had no clearly defined program for government. Accordingly, he pursued a set of dualistic policies designed to placate both his conservative allies and the hard-line elements within Fascism. In the year and a half after taking office, he made a number of concessions to his powerful allies in the state, industry, church, and conservative political camp. For example, as soon as he received the invitation to form a government, he immediately ordered the demobilization of the Fascist squads in Rome to reassure state authorities of his peaceful intentions. To bolster his support among Catholics and to weaken the opposition within the Popular party, the onetime anti-clerical firebrand wooed the Vatican and the conservative wing of Catholicism by introducing religious instruction into all state schools, banning obscene publications, and outlawing the sale of contraceptives. To appease powerful business interests, he appointed an orthodox liberal economist, Alberto De'Stefani, as minister of finance and proclaimed his government's commitment to "the greatest economic liberty" and a balanced budget. These reassuring words found confirmation in his treatment of the leading organization of Italian industrialists, *Confindustria*, which enjoyed steadily improving relations with the Fascist government in 1923. Mussolini also bolstered his support on the right by engineering a merger of the Fascist and Nationalist parties in early 1923 that brought into his party a more educated and upper-class contingent of right-wing monarchists and Catholics. More generally, he reassured proponents of normalcy by attempting to reduce the power of Fascist warlords and to reassert the authority of the prefects, the principal state officials at the provincial level.

At the same time, Mussolini also took steps to reassure the Fascists that he had not abandoned "the revolution" or sold out to the establishment. In his first address to the Chamber of Deputies in mid-November, he employed a tough language designed to appeal to the hard-line elements in his party and the paramilitary squads:

> Revolution has its rights and I am here to defend and develop the revolution of the Black Shirts. I refused to make an outright conquest as I could have done . . . . I might have made this bleak hall a bivouac for my platoons. I might have closed parliament altogether and created a government of Fascists alone. I could have done that, but such, at least for the present, has not been my wish.

In the following month, he further appeased the Fascist warlords by ordering the arrest of the Communist party leadership, and in the spring of 1923 the police jailed hundreds of local Communist organizers, forcing the party to go underground. In addition, Mussolini tacitly condoned a reign of extralegal terror by the squadrists against members of the opposition that resulted in an average of five assaults a day in 1923, with most carried out in broad daylight to maximize their effect. These irregular operations took on a more organized form in early 1924, when Mussolini set up a special squad, the *ceka*, to go after prominent antifascists.

In addition to the continued violence, the Duce created a series of new institutions to bolster his power and signal to his followers that he intended to transform drastically the political situation in Italy. In December 1922, he set up the Fascist Grand Council to coordinate the activities of the party and other Fascist organizations with those of the government. Significantly, Mussolini appointed the members of the Grand Council and personally decided when it met and what it discussed. One of the first acts of the Grand Council was to found a second new institution, the Voluntary Militia for National Security, a military force that provided the Duce with his own political police and an instrument "to defend the revolution of October 1922." As such, the Militia offered both a means of disciplining the unruly violence of the squadrists by putting them on the state payroll and a way of curbing the independence of the provincial warlords of fascism.

Mussolini's cultivation of Fascist hard-liners came in handy when he set out to reform Italy's electoral system in the summer of 1923 to strengthen his fragile base of support in parliament. His proposal, the so-called Acerbo bill, replaced the system of proportional representation with one in which the party that got the largest number of votes automatically received two-thirds of the seats in the Chamber of Deputies. Once again he skillfully combined conciliatory arguments and intimidation by armed Fascists to gain parliamentary support and the approval of the monarchy. Mussolini won over the elder statesmen of the constitutional camp with the promise that the reform would end the political instability, which had plagued the country since 1919, by guaranteeing a strong executive capable of restoring order. To discourage the opposition and win over those allies who remained unconvinced by his promises, he threatened to mobilize his Black Shirts for a "second wave" of terror and violence and toured the provinces to rally his supporters. When the bill came to a vote, Fascist militia maintained a menacing presence around the Chamber of Deputies. The combination of promises and threats was successful, and the electoral bill became law in July, virtually assuring Mussolini's government a safe parliamentary majority in any future election.

On the whole, the need to consolidate his power in Italy encouraged Mussolini to avoid any dramatic initiatives in foreign policy.

Nonetheless, he did appeal to nationalist elements by seeming, albeit briefly, to commit Italy to a more aggressive policy of "national greatness" through territorial expansion later in the summer of 1923 when an Italian general was killed in Greece. This event provided Mussolini with the pretext for the bombardment and military occupation of the Greek island of Corfu. Although diplomatic pressures from England forced him to withdraw from the island after a month, Mussolini managed to transform the Corfu crisis into an ideological victory both abroad and at home. Not only did his unilateral action against Greece raise Fascist Italy's profile at the expense of the international peacekeeping ambitions of the League of Nations, but it also received broad support from both the old guard and the general public at home because he seemed to be standing up for the Italian nation.

With his new electoral system in place and his popularity on the rise, Mussolini dissolved the parliament in January 1924 and called for new elections in the first week in April. From the outset, the government approached the vote not as an exercise in free choice by Italian citizens, but rather as an opportunity to demonstrate mass support for national unity, fascism, and the Duce's leadership. Accordingly, the Fascists mounted an aggressive propaganda campaign on behalf of the government's *listone*, or big electoral slate of Fascist candidates and their allies, which received generous financing from powerful industrialists. The disarray, divisions, and parochial concerns of the old moderate political parties led men of property throughout the country to join the Fascist-dominated list. Leaving nothing to chance, the government and Black Shirts used violence, police repression, and electoral fraud, especially outside the media gaze of the big cities, to weaken the opposition and to ensure the desired outcome. On the surface, the results marked a major triumph for the Duce and Fascists who provided two-thirds of the candidates in the *listone*. In fact, the government won the largest victory in the 83-year history of unified Italy, capturing 65 percent of the votes cast and automatically receiving 374 of the 535 seats in the new Chamber of Deputies.

The Fascists' success at the ballot box, however, also made it considerably more important for Mussolini to define the fundamental character and direction of Italian fascism. Once he had become prime minister after the March on Rome, Mussolini had relied upon his skills as a political manager to balance the conflicting obligations of restoring state power with the anti-state activism of the Fascist movement. He had managed to do so by combining two distinct roles: that of the prime minister of a coalition government and that of the Duce of an openly anti-democratic mass movement. In the wake of the elections of 1924, competition for office and the huge growth of the Fascist party, whose membership more than doubled in 1923, led to bitter conflicts between the "Fascists of the first hour" and more opportunistic but better educated recent converts. Party unity and the suppression of these rivalries became considerably less likely, since the opposition was in disarray and the conservative parties were largely moribund after the elections. While Mussolini's conservative allies in the "respectable" propertied classes, the monarchy, and the army were pressuring him to impose discipline on his party and put an end to the violent excesses of the squadrists, hard-line Fascists were demanding that he break definitively with the old order and finally carry out the "second wave of revolution." Dramatic developments in the summer of 1924 forced Mussolini to make the decisions that would lead to the emergence of a full-blown Fascist dictatorship.

I V

Architect of the
Totalitarian State

1924–1935

The transition of fascism from a constitutional governing party into a dictatorial regime was less the product of a carefully orchestrated plan of action than the outcome of a crisis that enveloped Mussolini and his government in the second half of 1924. The crisis began at the end of May when the prominent socialist leader Giacomo Matteotti gave a speech before the Chamber of Deputies, attacking Fascist electoral violence and fraud and demanding that the results of the vote be annulled. Adding fuel to the fire, Matteotti published an article a week later, in which he accused Mussolini's government of accepting bribes from American oil companies in exchange for drilling rights in Italy. Shortly thereafter, Mussolini reportedly told a member of the Fascist Grand Council that Matteotti "should no longer be in circulation." On June 10, a squad of thugs kidnapped and murdered the parliamentary deputy, a brutal and clumsy crime that rapidly unraveled. Witnesses got the license number of the car involved, and it led back to the Fascists. After Matteotti's body was found in a shallow grave outside Rome in mid-August, the police arrested five men from Mussolini's secretive antifascist squad, the *Ceka*, two of whom had close ties with the head of government, along with the car's owner and another Fascist who were charged as accessories.

While it remains unclear whether Mussolini intentionally commissioned the murder, the crime provoked an immediate public outcry against his government and party that initially seemed to threaten the very survival of fascism. The uproar clearly shook Mussolini's confidence. At first, he tried to distance himself from the crime by denouncing it in parliament and by promising to bring its perpetrators to justice. These gestures did little to placate the antifascist opposition, a polyglot of communists, socialists, and liberal democrats, who attacked the government as "unconstitutional" and walked out of the Chamber of Deputies in protest at the end of June. In an attempt to seize the moral high ground, they formed a separate assembly, the so-called

Aventine secession. Although this assembly had no real authority over the government, its very existence reflected the depth of opposition to Mussolini and his government.

To complicate matters for Mussolini, the killing also sparked simultaneous and irreconcilable challenges to his leadership both from his conservative supporters and from the Fascist hard-liners. The premeditated political murder of a parliamentary deputy proved too much for many respectable conservatives, both within the party and outside it. They demanded that Mussolini take decisive steps to restore law and order and to repress the chaotic violence of the squadrists once and for all. Four of his ministers threatened to resign unless he broadened the political base of the government and removed his most violent subordinates. To curry their favor, Mussolini not only sacrificed the perpetrators of the crime, but also relinquished his position as minister of interior to Luigi Federzoni, ex-Nationalist and a respected figure in royal and military circles. Such concessions, however, infuriated extremist elements within the party and militia, who reacted to the crisis by demanding that he unleash a violent offensive against all opposition forces, break definitively with the old constitutional order, and carry out the long-awaited "second wave" of Fascist revolution.

Mussolini had dealt with these contradictory pressures from conservatives and hard-liners before by alternating concessions, but this approach no longer seemed to work in the atmosphere of anger and distrust created by the Matteotti affair. To preserve his bargaining power and hold on to his official position, he set out to rally his mass base within the Fascist party by touring the provinces at the end of the summer of 1924. The Matteotti affair, however, had inspired the most turbulent Black Shirts in the provinces and the militia, who became increasingly unhappy with Mussolini's reluctance to act decisively. More alarmingly, they threatened to launch, with or without him, a new campaign of violence against all non-fascists. Mussolini could not permit such an undisciplined reign of terror by the hard-liners without risking the complete political isolation of fascism and the intervention of the king and the army to restore order. Accordingly, he distributed a circular to all party members at the end of November, in which he called for the conciliation of the government's allies, condemned illegal actions, and threatened a purge of "those who make violence a profession." Still, these initiatives did little to reassure his conservative allies or tame the hard-line elements in the provinces.

A variety of circumstances worked to Mussolini's advantage in December. To begin with, the decision of the Liberal, Communist, and Socialist parties to abandon parliament and create the Aventine secession dramatically narrowed the range of available solutions within the framework of the Italian constitution. Above all, the Aventine confronted the propertied classes and the representatives of Italy's established institutions with a choice between fascism and antifascism. The monarchy, the army, the Vatican, and important sectors of the business community all refused to abandon Mussolini when the only alternative remained a largely left-wing, antifascist opposition that included communists. In their view, the leader of fascism represented the only public figure capable of resolving the crisis without running the risks of civil war and revolution. For his part, Victor Emanuel III steadfastly refused to dismiss Mussolini or intervene forcefully in the political situation, while the army chiefs signaled their preference by providing the Fascist militia with war surplus rifles. In a similar vein, Pope Pius XI warned the Catholic Popular party against joining the "atheistic" communists in the Aventine secession. The Vatican press instead counseled the faithful to forgive the Duce, employing the homily "Let him who is without sin cast the stone." Although a few businessmen wavered in their support of the government after the murder, industrialists, on the whole, refused to support the Aventine opposition or call for Mussolini's resignation. For the most part, they continued to rely on the promise of a Fascist restoration of state authority that would ensure social order and guarantee production.

Even with the tacit support of the old establishment, Mussolini only made the leap into dictatorship when confronted with the threat of a revolt from within his own political camp. In late December, spokesmen for the Fascist hardliners gave the Duce an ultimatum that he "pursue a grandiose program [to eliminate the political opposition], as we hope, or we . . . will engage in battle." This threat, combined with a simultaneous violent offensive by provincial Fascists in Florence, Pisa, Bologna, and other north-central cities, forced Mussolini to act. On January 3, 1925, he launched an explicit challenge to the antifascist opposition in a speech to the Chamber of Deputies:

> I declare, in the presence of this assembly and that of the whole Italian people, that I, and I alone, assume the political, moral, and historic responsibility for everything that has happened . . . . If fascism has been a criminal association, I am the head of that association . . . . If all the acts of violence have been the result of a given historical, political, and moral climate, well then, mine is the responsibility . . . . When two irreducible elements are in conflict, the solution

is force . . . . You may be sure that within forty-eight hours from this speech of mine, the situation will be clarified all along the line.

In the wake of Mussolini's speech, the Fascist militia immediately mobilized. More than one hundred members of the opposition were arrested, homes were searched, "subversive" groups were disbanded, and the prefects were ordered to tighten controls on the press and crush any display of antifascism. The days that followed also witnessed the resignation of the remaining liberal ministers and their replacement by a new all-Fascist government, in which Mussolini occupied four ministerial posts in addition to the prime minister's office.

These developments marked the beginning of a four-year process of institutional transformation that would convert Italy's constitutional parliamentary state into a full-fledged Fascist dictatorship. This process had two principal projects: first, the "fascistization" of the old state apparatus, and second, the subordination of the Fascist party to the state. The first project involved the creation of a political and administrative system that assured all power to fascism. From the outset, Mussolini emerged as the central catalyst and most visible instrument of the state's transformation. Working long hours every day, he involved himself directly in the sweeping changes that took place in these years. Mussolini also skillfully exploited four separate assassination attempts between November 1925 and October 1926 to galvanize support. Hours after the second attempt by a deranged Irish woman in April 1926, for instance, a bandaged Mussolini urged his followers to "live dangerously" and told them, "If I go forward, follow me. If I retreat, kill me. If I die, avenge me." The assassination attempts aroused a mixture of fear and indignation that predisposed the Italian public to accept the dismantling of the old liberal parliamentary system.

As a result, Mussolini's executive authority greatly increased at the expense of the legislature, local government, and individual rights. To begin with, new laws banned all opposition parties, unions, and associations and required state employees to take an oath of allegiance to the government, effectively creating a one-party state. Other measures replaced elected mayors with state-appointed officials and expanded the powers of the prefects over provincial life. The last vestiges of the old constitutional order disappeared in 1929 with the closing of the Chamber elected in 1924 and its replacement by a non-elective body dominated by the Fascists. Additional measures tightened controls on the press, blocked clandestine emigration, increased police powers of internal exile that allowed the forced relocation of dissidents to isolated areas of the country, and reintroduced the death penalty for political crimes. As an ex-journalist, Mussolini took a particular interest in the regulation of the daily newspapers. He formed the Fascist Press Office to control public access to the news. The code of conduct that he imposed on the media extended well beyond political matters. Papers were expected to present an optimistic picture of Italian daily life and to avoid covering natural and economic disasters as well as stories about crime and personal tragedies.

To enforce these measures and intimidate opponents, Mussolini created a new position, "head of the government," that gave him full executive authority without recourse to parliament. In this role, he greatly increased the number of police officers and the levels of police control. He oversaw not only the regular police, but also the forces of the Fascist militia and the military police or Carabinieri, all of whom moved aggressively against any form of overt political protest or opposition. By 1930, these forces averaged 20,000 operations a week against enemies of the regime. Mussolini also met on a daily basis with the chief of a new secret police, the OVRA (Organization of Volunteers for the Repression of Antifascism), which maintained a network of informers, agents, and agents provocateurs to infiltrate real or perceived opposition groups, both at home and abroad. Operating behind a veil of institutional secrecy, the OVRA developed a huge data bank on political suspects and employed torture and coercion to extract confessions and inculcate a general climate of fear in the ranks of the discontented and the antifascists. In addition to these extensive police powers, Mussolini also employed after 1926 a new judicial body, the Special Tribunal for the Defense of the Fascist State, to punish his enemies. Staffed by military men and members of the Fascist militia, this court handed down more than 13,000 convictions against "political criminals" during the ensuing 16 years.

Mussolini also used his repressive apparatus against the legendary Sicilian criminal organization, the Mafia, which he viewed as a threat to his absolute authority. In the fall of 1925, he appointed an especially tough prefect, Cesare Mori, to the post in Palermo. Mori immediately carried out a wave of mass arrests of known or suspected mafiosi. He threatened to jail the wives and children of those men who escaped the dragnet unless they turned themselves in. During the following two years, a series of show trials concluded with lengthy sentences for virtually all the defendants. These harsh measures did not touch the underlying structural roots of organized crime, but they did have the desired effect of virtually eliminating Mafia activity.

The second dimension of the political transformation that took place in the latter half of the 1920s involved the taming of the Fascist party and the gradual subordination of its provincial chiefs and activists to the authority of the Duce and the state. Mussolini's decisive break with the constitutional political order in 1925 had initially appeared to mark a great victory for the hard-line advocates of the "second wave," whose leading spokesman, Roberto Farinacci, took over as secretary of the Fascist party. However, the Duce's distrust of overly independent Fascist warlords and his preference for a more disciplined police state ultimately spelled defeat for the ambitions of the black-shirted militants to forge a genuine party-state. For his part, the authoritarian Farinacci contributed to the process of centralization by imposing a rigid conformity on the provincial Fascists at the same time that he expanded the powers of the national party leadership and bureaucracy. Newly appointed party administrators, the *federali*, took charge of the local *fasci* and disbanded the punitive squads. Farinacci's successor, Augusto Turati, followed suit by expelling violent troublemakers and overseeing a massive admission of

new members drawn from the ranks of the professional classes and white-collar employees.
Many Fascists of the first hour received jobs
within the expanding state administration; those
who refused to get with the program fell victim
to the same police repression that hammered the
regime's antifascist opponents. As a result of
these measures, after 1928 Mussolini could rely
on the apolitical prefects to control the Fascist
party, which then became an obedient instrument
of state policy and an avenue for social advancement and employment for its members. The
process concluded at the end of that year when
the party's chief governing body, the Fascist
Grand Council, became an official state organ,
presided over by the head of the government. As
the decade came to an end, Mussolini had laid
the foundations for his personal supremacy over
both the Italian state and his movement.

The Duce's aspirations for fascism went beyond the creation of a police state capable of
guaranteeing public order and ruthlessly repressing all forms of political dissent. Indeed, what
most distinguished Mussolini from traditional
authoritarian conservatives was his aspiration to
create a "totalitarian" regime that penetrated
into virtually all areas of everyday social and private life. He captured the essence of this desire in
the slogan "All within the state, nothing outside

the state, nothing against the state." In this fashion, he hoped to "bring the masses into the state" as a disciplined and enthusiastic base of support for the regime. To achieve his objectives, the regime introduced an extremely ambitious array of new social and cultural programs and organizations that touched the ostensibly apolitical arenas of culture, sexuality, family, and social welfare in the 1930s. In each of these arenas, Mussolini and his officials oversaw new mass initiatives that aspired to promote national consciousness and undermine old class and regional loyalties by regrouping people on the basis of sex, age, activity, and social group.

From the outset, the Duce paid particular attention to the education of the younger generation growing up under fascism. At the symbolic level, the "Roman" salute became compulsory in Italian schools in December 1925, and in the following year the regime proclaimed the anniversary of the March on Rome as an official day of "national rejoicing." In the second half of the decade, Mussolini set out to conquer and transform the country's school system in a direction that served the political objectives of fascism. As a first step, the regime attacked the independence of the teachers by purging their ranks of those under suspicion of antifascist sympathies in 1926 and then by increasing the authority of headmasters, principals, and other school supervisors to monitor the ideological views of teachers and students and to promote staff according to political criteria. To "fascistize" the content of the educational system, the regime also carried out a sweeping purge of the old textbooks and introduced in their place a single state-approved textbook in 1928–1929. The resulting Fascist educational curriculum served principally as a mechanism of political indoctrination with every subject tailored to the needs of the regime. Thus the new official history textbook, for example, linked fascism and its mission of expansion to the glories of ancient Rome and Italian national unification, while playing down the importance of Renaissance individualism and nineteenth-century liberalism in the country's development.

At the same time, Mussolini and the Fascist regime attempted to shape and regiment the lives of young people outside the classroom. They did so by creating new state-sponsored youth organizations, resembling the Boy Scouts, that operated under the umbrella of the Opera Nazionale Balilla (ONB). In this fashion Mussolini pioneered a strategy that Nazi Germany and other nation-states would follow in the 1930s to foster more intense national loyalties in their citizens. The ONB, which enjoyed an official monopoly of youth activities in 1928, oversaw four organizations: the

Balilla for boys between the ages of eight and fifteen, the *Avanguardie* for boys fifteen to eighteen, and the *piccole italiane* and *giovani italiane* for girls in these age groups. With staffs drawn from the ranks of Fascist teachers and militia members, these organizations provided semi-military training for Italian boys in the form of drills, gymnastics, and sports. In addition, they arranged excursions, camping trips, lectures, and ceremonial rituals. All of these activities served as vehicles of political indoctrination that stressed the Fascist virtues of discipline, obedience, comradeship, and order. The organizations for Italian girls had a somewhat different mission, namely to promote the values of motherhood and family. Accordingly, their activities included courses on first aid, charity, child care, and handicrafts. While membership in all of these youth groups remained voluntary in theory, encouragement from Fascist teachers and preferential access to scholarships, prizes, and other perks helped attract nearly 3.5 million youths to the ONB by the mid-1930s.

As the distinctive missions of the youth organizations for boys and girls suggest, Mussolini's regime aspired to mold the private behavior of men and women in a decidedly traditionalist direction through the relentless glorification of home and hearth, patriarchal authority, and childbearing. To a certain extent, Fascist sexual policies reflected a wider European preoccupation in the early twentieth century with declining fertility and growing job competition between men and women. The regime viewed falling birthrates, in particular, as a threat to national strength and responded by attempting to change the reproductive behavior of Italians. To improve national fertility rates, Fascist authorities banned abortions, outlawed contraceptives and sexual education courses, and introduced a variety of incentives and penalties to exclude women from the work force and encourage them and their spouses to have more children. Fathers of large families, for instance, received tax breaks and preferential treatment in the distribution of housing and jobs, while prizes were awarded in each city to the most prolific women. In 1933, Mussolini personally greeted the 93 female winners, who between them had given birth to 1,300 children.

Mussolini's regime also provided some real benefits to women who had enjoyed very little social assistance from the Italian state in the past. A new para-state agency, ONMI (National Institute for Maternity and Infancy), launched an aggressive propaganda blitz to exalt the importance of maternity and motherhood for the welfare and strength of the nation and to promote the virtues of breast-feeding and modern child-rearing practices. ONMI took control of "all private and public institutions for the assistance and protection of motherhood and infancy" in the second half of the 1920s. In this capacity, it attempted to develop a variety of educational, medical, health, and welfare programs for needy mothers, infants, and children. By 1930, ONMI had created 130 new mixed maternal and infant clinics that assisted hundreds of thousands of Italian women.

At the same time that fascism glorified women's roles in the home and the nursery and their subordination to men, the totalitarian ambitions of the regime also led it to mobilize its female subjects on behalf of the Duce and the nation. To achieve this objective, new organizations emerged in the 1930s with activities that drew women away from their homes and into the public arena. When the regime launched its campaign of "social reclamation" of the poor, for instance, women became the front-line forces as *visitatrici fasciste,* or volunteers, who worked directly with the needy. In a similar vein, the authorities involved women's groups as highly visible participants in the great mass rallies and public demonstrations of the 1930s in support of the regime's initiatives. In the process, millions of Italian women left their domestic enclaves, at least temporarily, to take part in the public rituals and activities of the Fascist party's female auxiliaries.

The regime's preoccupation with social control, national strength, and efficiency inspired fascism's other social welfare programs and policies. The Fascist welfare state that emerged in the 1930s introduced a host of new programs of social insurance against illness, unemployment, accidents, and old age. With its funds for jobless subsidies, disability, maternity insurance, and pensions for the elderly, the new National Social Insurance Institute, for example, gave Mussolini's regime a very powerful instrument of control over segments of Italian society that had been previously untouched by the state. Access to these benefits presupposed participation in the organizational life of the regime, allowing Fascist authorities to use political loyalty rather than social justice concerns to determine inclusion and exclusion. In a similar vein, the regime used its monopoly of other scarce resources such as housing, jobs, and schools to permeate virtually all areas of everyday life, rewarding those who conformed to the commands of the dictatorship.

Mussolini also initiated an ambitious program of public work projects to provide jobs and leave fascism's permanent mark on the Italian landscape. In the years after 1925, the regime undertook the construction of hundreds of bridges, thousands of miles of new roads, and giant aqueducts that brought water to previously arid regions. The same years saw the regime drain and reclaim hundreds of thousands of acres of marshland throughout the country. The crowning achievement of the campaign was the draining of 150,000 acres of the malarial swamps surrounding Rome and their transformation into an area of new towns and small peasant landholdings.

Mussolini's totalitarian aspirations extended well beyond the material needs of the population. His regime also set out to organize and control the consumer habits and leisure-time activities of the Italian people. The *Opera Nazionale Dopolavoro*, or the National After-Work Foundation, took the lead in this ambitious campaign of ideological and social persuasion. This organization incorporated two sections, one for industrial workers and another for white-collar employees. To promote a heightened national consciousness and enthusiastic support for fascism, the 20,000 recreational circles of the *Dopolavoro* sponsored a wide range of activities and initiatives. By the end of the 1930s, they ran thousands of theaters, movie houses, orchestras, and libraries as well as more than 11,000 sporting groups. Members received discounts and access to group events that exposed them to new forms of mass media and commercial entertainment such as the radio and movies. The *Dopolavoro* also organized outings and tourist trips for ordinary Italians as a way to erode tenacious local loyalties and replace them with a new national identity inseparably tied to the Duce and fascism. Similarly, the leisure-time organizations attempted to appropriate traditional pastimes and forms of popular recreation and harness them to the needs and objectives of the regime. They encouraged, in particular, "games of pure Italian origin" that emphasized team discipline and group solidarity, while nourishing in the participants a shared sense of national identity.

Mussolini's regime was especially innovative in its propagandistic and political use of sports, both as popular participatory activities and as mass spectator events. In their enthusiastic promotion of sports at the popular level, Fascist authorities had one clear objective: the formation of a new generation of strong, fit, virile, and disciplined young Italian men ready and willing to serve the nation and the regime in the workplace and on the battlefield. The youth groups tied to the ONB became the principal means for organizing sports and competitive activities on a massive scale. Under government auspices, new academies trained an armada of sports instructors, gym teachers, and coaches to provide physical and sports education to millions of young Italians. The regime also invested heavily in the construction of outdoor sports facilities and gyms. By 1930, more than 3,000 facilities were either available or under construction. Six years later, 3.7 million members of the ONB were taking part in organized sports at some 5,000 athletic centers across the country.

Mussolini stands out as the first dictator to use the resources of the state to promote the success of his country's elite athletes in international competitions. He recognized that victories provided invaluable political propaganda for the Fascist regime. Not only did they bring glory to fascism and enhance its prestige abroad, but they also aroused national pride and patriotic devotion at home. In this respect, the Duce pioneered a model for the state-sponsored sports programs of Nazi Germany in the 1930s and the Soviet Bloc countries after 1945. With the backing of the state, the country's athletes enjoyed a remarkable string of international successes after 1930, making the ensuing decade a golden age for Italian sports. At the Olympic Games of 1932 in Los Angeles, the Italian team paid homage to fascism at the opening ceremonies before going on to win more medals than any other nation with the exception of the host U.S. squad. In the following year, a giant Italian immigrant to the United States, Primo Carnera, won the world's heavyweight boxing title. Italian teams enjoyed even greater success on the soccer fields, winning two World Cups in 1934 and 1938 as well as the Olympic title in 1936. Finally, the decade of the 1930s also witnessed the emergence of a number of great Italian cyclists, including Gino Bartoli, winner of the Tour de France in 1938. Not surprisingly, Mussolini enthusiastically embraced and promoted these achievements for his own purposes. In the hands of his propagandists, the nation's sports heroes and their athletic triumphs became tangible embodiments of Fascist Italy's general superiority over other nations and political systems in the competitive international arena.

Increasingly, Fascist authorities also promoted sports as part of a campaign to make Italians into a nation of spectators and fans. In the midst of the Great Depression, major athletic events served as a new form of mass entertainment that distracted people from the economic hardships and uncertainties of the period. The regime actively encouraged the growth of professional sports, bankrolling the construction of vast public soccer stadiums in the major cities, granting tax incentives to sports entrepreneurs, and subsidizing the travel of professional teams. To expand further the ranks of the sporting public, the state also began to transmit radio broadcasts of soccer matches and other athletic competitions. While the radio remained too expensive a purchase for the majority of Italians in the 1930s, millions became avid fans of their favorite teams by listening to the matches in public settings offered by bars, cafes, and Fascist party sections and clubs.

Perhaps the most ambitious project of the totalitarian state, however, involved efforts by the party to make fascism a national secular religion that would transform the character of the Italian people. Indeed, Mussolini's regime was the first European state since the French Revolution to attempt such a project, and in doing so it provided a model for the Nazi regime and Soviet Stalinists in the 1930s. Fascism's high priests envisioned a new civic religion capable of instilling in Italians an unquestioning faith in its doctrines, absolute obedience to its commandments, and a manly dedication to the nation it embodied. In pursuit of these objectives, Mussolini's regime devoted an enormous amount of time, money, and manpower to the organization and promotion of new mass rites and rituals. As the Duce told a German journalist in the early 1930s, "Every revolution creates new forms, new myths, and new rites; the would-be revolutionist, while using old traditions, must refashion them. He must create new festivals, new gestures, new forms."

As a result, millions of Italians either partici-
pated in or viewed a seemingly endless round of
political ceremonies, rallies, parades, and pilgrimages. Party officials choreographed these
mass spectacles as highly theatrical, visual experiences that made extensive use of uniforms,
badges, banners, salutes, slogans, and songs to
galvanize both participants and spectators. They
aimed, first of all, to stimulate feelings of collective enthusiasm, commitment, and national community in the participants, who came from the
ranks of the Fascist mass organizations. At the
same time, the spectacles were designed to impress, inspire, and intimidate onlookers, or those
who saw newsreels and photos of the events,
with the majesty, power, unity, and efficiency of
the regime.

Such collective spectacles followed a schedule
dictated by the regime's new calendar, which
designated 1923 as year one of the Fascist era.
The government and party celebrated a host of
holidays, commemorating the founding of Rome,
national unification, the monarchy, important
anniversaries of the regime and its triumphs as
well as ceremonies honoring heroes and martyrs
of the Great War and the "Fascist Revolution."
The events celebrating the anniversary of the
March on Rome on October 28 displayed the essential features of these mass spectacles that

aimed to instill Fascist beliefs in the Italian people. In the morning, the regime organized memorial services and imposing military parades, involving uniformed members from all the Fascist mass organizations and veterans groups, who also made ceremonial pilgrimages to monuments honoring "the fallen" in the Great War and during the Fascist rise to power. Festive events took place in the afternoon with the population dancing, singing, and listening to musical entertainment in the public squares and streets, amid the flags, banners, and other symbols of the regime. On other occasions, party organizers appropriated traditional religious holidays on behalf of the state. The "Fascist Epiphany," for example, became a moment during the Christmas season when the authorities distributed gifts to poor children to demonstrate "the affectionate care of their Fascist nation."

Mussolini's regime also imposed its principal messages on a more permanent basis through its control and restructuring of public spaces in Italian cities. The massive new government buildings and monuments that arose after 1925 displayed the visual symbols and distinctive slogans of fascism on their facades. These structures provided citizens with a daily reminder of the power of the regime and associated fascism both with the forces of modernity and with the glories of

Italy's past. The reshaping of the country's urban landscape found its fullest expression in the rebuilding of Rome as the home of the "Fascist Revolution." According to the Duce, the capital had to become "a marvel to the nations of the world: vast, orderly, powerful, as it was in the times of the Augustan Empire." The 1930s witnessed the destruction of many older medieval neighborhoods in the city associated with the "centuries of decadence." In their place arose widened avenues and new Fascist headquarters, post offices, sports arenas, and government offices. These Fascist "temples" were all built on a scale and with an architectural style designed to reinforce the image of the regime as a dynamic, modernizing force. In a similar vein, the government oversaw the creation of new middle-class neighborhoods to accommodate the mass of people employed in the greatly enlarged state bureaucracy. By the end of the decade, Rome had doubled in size. Fascist propagandists touted the resulting benefits in terms of the improvements in traffic, housing, and hygiene as well as the tens of thousands of new jobs created by the construction projects. At the same time, the transformation of the capital in these years also emphasized the recovery and restoration of Imperial Rome, whose principal sites became venues for the regime's choreographed mass spectacles. In this fashion, the regime attempted to identify itself in the public mind with an era when the Italian peninsula had dominated the western world.

To what extent did this imposing array of social and cultural programs and initiatives succeed in winning over the hearts and minds of the Italian people for the cause of fascism? Mussolini's regime did manage to reach social groups who in the past had had virtually no contact with the Italian state. Moreover, some groups, especially the middle classes and the ranks of white-collar employees, benefited tangibly from Fascist policies in the form of preferential treatment, economic gains, and improvements in social status and prestige. Many of the same groups were also grateful to a regime that had apparently succeeded in imposing law and order and in ushering in a national resurgence after the chaos of the postwar years. On the whole, most Italians in the late twenties and early thirties appeared to have quietly reconciled themselves to the realities of life under the dictatorship. Referendums in 1929 and again in 1934, for instance, gave massive support to the regime and its policies.

Nonetheless, the heavily promoted campaigns and picturesque rituals of the totalitarian state did not produce any enduring mass enthusiasm for fascism, let alone a profound transformation in the attitudes and values of most Italians. From the outset, the regime's ambitious social projects lacked the money and planning skills to coordinate or deliver adequately the services their promoters had promised. To make matters worse, the highly centralized orchestration of Fascist rites and rituals encouraged rigid conformity and obedience at the expense of local initiatives or spontaneous displays of enthusiasm. As a result, such events tended to generate only a superficial emotional commitment to the regime on the part of many participants, who either went passively through the motions or else took part solely to advance personal career ambitions. Already by 1932, large segments of the public were viewing the Fascist mass spectacles with increasing apathy, skepticism, impatience, and even ridicule, forcing organizational leaders to rely on various forms of coercion to ensure the participation of their members.

The inability of the totalitarian campaigns to transform Italian society did little to diminish the seemingly genuine popularity and adulation enjoyed by Mussolini, however. On the contrary, the failure of the regime and party to establish enduring structures of social mobilization and active consensus only strengthened the personal charismatic authority of the Duce and magnified his pivotal role within the dictatorship. In fact, the entire system created by the regime in the years after 1925 depended increasingly upon his decisions and initiatives. Mussolini became inseparably linked to fascism in the public mind, and the Duce emerged as "the Leader of Fascism, the Guide, the Supreme Head of the Regime."

V

Mussolini and the Cult of the Duce

1925–1938

As the decade of the 1920s came to a close, Benito Mussolini had already amassed a level of personal institutional power within Italy that would remain without parallel in the years between the two world wars. In contrast to his German counterpart, Adolf Hitler, who preferred to delegate authority to competent subordinates, the Duce himself assumed an amazing number of official positions and responsibilities in the Fascist regime. By the early 1930s, he not only served as head of the government, but he also occupied eight cabinet posts that put him directly in charge of the ministries of foreign affairs, interior, colonies, war, navy, aviation, public works, and corporations. During the same years, he also presided over the Fascist party and the Fascist Grand Council, served as commandant general of the Fascist militia, and chaired seven other important state councils.

Mussolini was a hardworking executive with a fine memory for details. Despite all his responsibilities, he insisted on making all major policy decisions and was even known to take an interest in minor administrative matters. As a result, virtually everything that happened in the areas of government and legislation increasingly depended upon him. At the same time, he took steps to preclude any challenges to his authority from within fascism. Thus, he carried out frequent rotations of officeholders and gradually moved his most prominent and able collaborators from the early Fascist movement to "honorary" positions that kept them at the margins of power within the dictatorship. In a similar fashion, the purges of the independent militants "of the first hour" and the massive recruitment campaigns transformed the Fascist party into an organization filled with members whose principal loyalties were to Mussolini rather than to the original movement.

The Duce's extraordinary place in the Fascist regime rested not only on his control of institutional power, but also on his role as a charismatic leader who enjoyed a mystical bond with the Italian people. Indeed, the burgeoning "cult of the Duce" that developed around Mussolini represented arguably the most innovative feature of the Italian dictatorship. With the passage of time, this cult, a form of ritualized exaltation of and devotion to the leader, became the one great unifying element of the regime and the ultimate guarantor of its survival and cohesion. More importantly, the cult of the Duce had a profound international resonance, serving as a prototype for Hitler's "Führer" cult in Nazi Germany as well as for the personality cults employed by populist dictators in Latin America, Asia, the Middle East, and Africa after World War II.

The qualities attributed to Mussolini by Fascist propagandists in the 1930s certainly conformed to the definition of the charismatic leader advanced by the German sociologist Max Weber. According to Weber, charismatic leaders are distinguished by certain personality traits that set them apart from "ordinary men" and seem to endow them "with supernatural, superhuman, or at least specifically exceptional powers or qualities." The Fascist cult of the Duce rested, in large part, on the image of Mussolini as an all-powerful, all-knowing, omnipresent prophet, savior, creator, and guide to the nation. Fittingly, the central slogan of the regime became "The Duce is always right." The Fascist press portrayed him as a great man "sent by God to

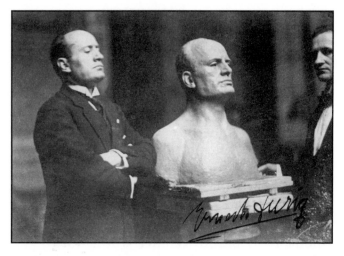

The forging of the cult of the Duce in the 1920s

Italy," the "divine Caesar," and the "sublime redeemer," in possession of magical powers. In this
guise, he stood out as a dynamic and thoroughly
modern "man of the people," who harnessed the
power of the new technology to take his country
into the future, while simultaneously restoring
the reassuring old values of the nation, family,
faith, and soil. Mussolini embodied the strong
but loving father figure who watched over his
people and saw everything, guaranteeing them
peace, order, and prosperity at home and national greatness abroad. He alone deserved
credit for all the benefits provided by fascism,

from "making the trains run on time" to draining the swamps and raising the country's international prestige. For exponents of the cult, he
accomplished all these wonders because he was a
man of genius and infallible judgment, with a
knowledge of all intellectual and artistic fields,
who worked around the clock and miraculously
seemed to be in several places at once.

While similar attributes were ascribed to Hitler
and Stalin by their followers, the Fascist cult of
the Duce also required that Mussolini himself become a poster boy for his people, incarnating in
his physical presence and actions all the virtues of
the new Italian. His propagandists ceaselessly
touted his qualities of strength, discipline,
courage, virility, and stamina, pointing to his tire-
less work habits, his love of sports and dangerous
activities, his sexual prowess, and his perpetually
youthful appearance. Such qualities were supposed to provide an inspirational "living and
working model" to all Italians of what they could
and should be. Above all, the idealized figure of
Mussolini was held out as an inspiration to the
younger generation whose entire lives had taken
place under the regime. Thus Fascist propagandists constantly urged Italian children and adoles-
cents to model themselves and their actions "on
the living example of the DUCE," since he was
"the finest, the strongest, the best of the sons" of

Italy. Even his "simple, clear, masculine" style of speaking and writing served as the model for the correct "Fascist" Italian that the schools and the press disseminated to the larger public.

The cult of the Duce took advantage of Mussolini's own larger-than-life personality and his distinctive talents. As a very young man, he was driven by a need to "become a man out of the ordinary" and "to engrave a mark in time with my will, like a lion does with his claw." Both his enemies and his supporters recognized that he possessed a powerful personal magnetism. In his early days in the Socialist movement, his physical appearance impressed supporters and acquaintances, who often commented on his dark eyes, riveting gaze, thick lips, powerful jaw, and barrel chest. The link between the physical and the political emerged with striking clarity in the comments of one female enthusiast. In 1913 she wrote how Mussolini was "the Socialist for heroic times. He still feels, he still believes, and his feelings and beliefs are endowed with a virile, forceful élan. He is a man." In a similar vein, a hometown friend depicted him two years later as a "force of nature" and a "man of action par excellence." Even his critics conceded that he possessed a tremendous vitality and quick intelligence and could charm and impress those with whom he had direct contact.

Mussolini's talents as a stage manager, performer, and orator allowed him to take full advantage of his physical assets and personal charisma. As the great Italian playwright Luigi Pirandello observed, the Duce was a "true man of the theater" and therefore particularly well suited to an era in which new forms of mass media were emerging. He and his subordinates carefully orchestrated all of his encounters with the public to magnify the impact of his physicality, voice, and oratorical skills. Mussolini was the first Italian leader to "go to the people." He traveled throughout Italy, making speeches in which he choreographed his facial expressions and physical gestures to his words. He delivered his speeches to the public with a distinctive cadence that conveyed the desired messages of strength and confidence.

The cult of the Duce benefited from postwar conditions and a number of developments in the 1920s. The parliamentary paralysis, social disorder, and economic difficulties of the first years after the Great War greatly enhanced the popular appeal of a youthful and energetic politician like Mussolini who projected the image of a "strong man" capable of rescuing the nation, restoring stability, and leading the Italian people into a glorious new era. Even before the Fascists had come to power, astute observers like the liberal senator Giustino Fortunato warned the public of impending civil war and noted how "everyone is invoking, as in any time of extreme danger, the providential intervention of a Man with a capital 'M' who will know how to impose order on the nation." The March on Rome in October 1922 dramatically raised Mussolini's personal prestige both within his movement and in the country at large. Once in office, his youthfulness, turbulent life, and humble origins reinforced his image as a new type of leader.

These characteristics made him stand out from all previous prime ministers, who had been visibly older and decidedly more genteel and aloof in their personal style and social background. Mussolini exploited these differences in his tours to the provinces and in his frequent speeches to mass rallies. The forceful manner in which the Duce imposed his dictatorship on the Italian people between 1925 and 1929 further exalted his image as an "exceptional man on whom history has conferred the task of creating the new order." In addition, Mussolini's seemingly miraculous ability to survive repeated assassination attempts in 1925 and 1926 enhanced his aura as a superman "protected by God." Only hours after the second attempt on his life, for instance, the bandaged leader assured the crowds in front of his offices that he was "the newest sort of Italian, one who is never thrown by events but rather proceeds always straight down the road assigned by destiny."

The cult of the Duce, however, was not simply a natural outgrowth of Mussolini's larger-than-life personality or the result of fortuitous circumstances. It was also the carefully marketed product of one of the first great public relations/advertising campaigns of the twentieth century, a campaign that mobilized all the institutions and resources of the Fascist regime for its construction and promotion. From the outset, this campaign depended upon the existence of a police state with the means to repress the free circulation of information and to control public opinion in the country. Yet the real novelty of the cult lay in its efforts to move beyond the mere repression of antifascist views or criticism of Mussolini. Significantly, Fascist propagandists conceived of the Duce as a commodity to be aggressively marketed to citizen-consumers "by the same advertising and promotional techniques" employed in industry and commerce. Giuseppe Bottai, one of the key figures in the regime, made the point explicitly in 1930 when he observed:

> In mass politics, awareness of the leaders can only be achieved by broad strokes, with means designed to impress millions of imaginations and hearts. It is necessary to impose the face, the words, with photographic, cinematic, audio repetition. Repetition, repetition, repetition. Just like in commercial advertising.

As Bottai's comments suggest, the regime aimed to enlist all available means of communication to sell Mussolini to the Italian public as their all-knowing, ever-present, and all-powerful leader. Accordingly, Fascist publicists and propagandists made certain that newspapers, magazines, photographs, phonograph records, stamps, radio broadcasts, and newsreels made the Duce a constant and overwhelming presence in the daily lives of ordinary citizens.

The print media emerged as one of the first major arenas for the promotion of the cult of the Duce. As a former professional journalist and editor, Mussolini took a special interest in the press and moved aggressively after 1925 to tighten his control of newspapers and magazines through the Fascist Press Office. He played a direct role in the actual planning and presentation of the news, which always kept the floodlight on him, relentlessly exalting the Duce's image and achievements over and above the party and the regime. Achille Starace, head of the Fascist party in the 1930s, expressed the duty of the press in no uncertain terms: "one man and one man alone must be allowed to dominate the news every day, and the others must take pride in serving him in silence." As a more critical foreign commentator noted in the mid-1930s, "It is interesting, when it is not too nauseating, to observe how Mussolini fills the front page, the back page, and the middle pages" of Italian papers. When Italo Balbo, one of the leading figures in the Fascist movement and a legendary airplane pilot, completed the first round-trip solo flight between Rome and Chicago, the Italian press reported the event as "*The Wings of Mussolini* under the guidance of Balbo" and made it appear that the Duce bore principal responsibility for his success. One of the editors of *Il Popolo d'Italia* exemplified the adulatory tone of the press treatment of the Duce in 1934:

> He sees, he foresees, he senses, measures, acts, wills . . . . He tames fortune, masters destiny. He has dominated the most perilous situations, he has released the spark from nothing, has arrested and deviated the stream of history. He has created a people. He has aroused a Nation. He has organized a State, has fused a block of will, of hearts, of souls, of power. Everything takes breath and movement from Him, because it is He, the Hero . . . .

In this fashion, the press ensured that Mussolini received all the credit for every achievement and benefit attributed to fascism, while failures or problems were attributed to his underlings.

Architects of the cult overlooked no detail in crafting the Duce's image in the press. In order to reinforce the idea of his perpetual youth and virility, the newspapers gave extensive coverage of Mussolini's supposedly active participation in vigorous, risky sports and activities such as horseback riding, flying, and motorcycling. Conversely, they carefully avoided any mention of his illnesses, birthdays, or even of the fact that he wore glasses or had become a grandfather. Similar motives led the press to avoid accounts of his family life, but not stories of his amorous adventures. Mussolini displayed an equal concern with his image in the print media outside of Italy. He lavished attention on the foreign press corps, granting lengthy interviews to sympathetic or potentially friendly journalists. Their favorable portraits then became additional testimonials that might convince Italians of the universal admiration the Duce enjoyed abroad. At the same time, Mussolini personally oversaw the work of his press censors, who immediately confiscated any negative or critical foreign news reports.

The regime's preoccupation with the printed word also extended to the schools, which provided powerful instruments to promote the cult of the Duce. Teachers received strict instructions to glorify Mussolini's superior qualities and to integrate him and his achievements into their study plans. First-graders learned to read and write by memorizing and copying slogans like "Long live the DUCE, our Chief and the Founder of Fascism." Once students could read, their elementary school textbooks provided them with the message that "Benito Mussolini loves the children very much. The children of Italy love the Duce very much. Long live the Duce!" After school, students encountered the same messages in the form of graffiti painted on walls and etched into the facades of public buildings throughout the country. In addition to the slogans, students read carefully tailored biographies of the leader that highlighted his roles as "the Child Prodigy," war hero, and statesman to whom "the whole world listens in fear and admiration." Likewise, history texts used in the primary schools encouraged unquestioning faith in Mussolini by focusing on his leading role in the pantheon of heroes and great men in the Italian past. Even mathematics textbooks were enlisted in the campaign; fifth-grade students wrestled with problems like "If Mussolini earned 56 lire per month as a teacher, how much did he earn per day?"

The relative poverty of the country limited the effectiveness of the print media in promoting the cult of the Duce, however. A third of the population still could not read or write in the 1920s, while even more were only semiliterate. To reach these people, the party and the regime made extensive use of increasingly available visual and audio means of communication such as film and radio to spread their message. For Mussolini, these instruments had the added benefit of exploiting more fully his powerful physical presence as well as his undeniable gifts as an actor and orator. Indeed, the media allowed him to monopolize and saturate public and private space in an unprecedented fashion.

Above all, Mussolini's performances at huge mass rallies and other public ceremonies offered one of the most visible and highly publicized means of exalting the Duce's status and of establishing a direct connection between him and the Italian people. Despite the appearance of spontaneity, extensive preparation went into these carefully choreographed events. With an elevated balcony serving as his stage, Mussolini showed himself to the people, every physical gesture and facial expression calculated to reinforce his image as the all-powerful Duce. Typically, his rousing speeches were a succession of sound bites—simple statements, using a basic vocabulary, but delivered in an aggressive, confident tone. To give the crowds a sense of participation and the impression that he heard their concerns, he engaged in dialogues with them. He would ask them ritualized questions, to which they would respond with ritualized answers. An enthusiastic account of a rally in Rome in 1932 captured much of the staged character of these ceremonial events and their glorification of the Duce:

Squadrons of airplanes fly in ever-tighter circles overhead, as if to crown this splendid assembly . . . . The crowd continues to swell. The square is thronged. Fifty thousand people are there waiting for Mussolini, fifty thousand shout his name . . . . Every eye is fixed on the balcony where the Duce will appear . . . . It is twenty past six. The balcony doors open. Starace appears, waving the flag on its staff. The long wait is about to be rewarded, and indeed a huge cry breaks out in the square: "Long live the Duce!" . . . In the great embrasure of the window his profile appears, giving the Roman salute. He wears the uniform of an honorary corporal of the Militia and his head is bare. His eyes dwell on the crowd; the crowd quivers with excitement. "Duce, Duce!" The cry is infinitely multiplied over the clanging of the music. The event takes on the dimension of a huge, ritual declaration of faith. A whole people is exalted by One Man, it sees itself in Him. Then there are shouts of "Attention!" . . . It is now twenty-five past. Mussolini speaks to the people of Rome, to Italy.

These rituals of devotion to the Duce were not limited to the huge mass rallies. Increasingly, all anniversaries and commemorative ceremonies, including the unveiling of his portraits and busts in the public squares of Italy, became occasions to glorify Mussolini's infallible leadership and to display popular adoration of him. In fact, all meetings after 1931 began with an obligatory "salute to the Duce."

The Fascists enormously magnified the impact of mass rallies and other ceremonies beyond the people who were physically present by exploiting the new means of mass communications. The regime began in the mid-1930s to transmit the Duce's speeches over the radio to a much larger national audience. As a result, millions of Italians could hear Mussolini's voice in homes, schools, and other public venues, magnifying the impact of his performances. As one enthusiastic supporter observed, "We can no longer repeat the lament, 'I wasn't there,' because now the radio takes us there to the rally, bringing to us his words, his breathing, his tone, and the eager attention of the crowd." The regime also took advantage of the newsreels and documentaries that had to be shown before every movie in Italian theaters by repeatedly broadcasting the images, words, and actions of the Duce to audiences at home and abroad.

On a day-to-day basis, the cult of the Duce found its fullest expression in the flood of photographic images of Mussolini that already saturated the country even before 1925. In the following years, an estimated 30 million pictures circulated through the press and on postcards. Featuring the Duce in literally thousands of different outfits, poses, and situations, these images gave him an overwhelming visibility throughout

Italy. Such omnipresence struck one foreign correspondent with particular force during a visit to Rome in 1929:

> The image of the Duce is part of the existence; it directs all circumstances of Italian life . . . . He dominates the counter, presides over traffic, witnesses the civic activities of the merchant. It is the same at the station, on the bus, or at the dentist's . . . . Wherever you look, wherever you walk, you will find Mussolini, still Mussolini, always Mussolini.

Mussolini's portrait not only appeared in all public buildings, classrooms, and offices, but also it became a part of private interior decor, hanging on the walls of homes next to pictures of patron saints and other religious icons.

Much like every other aspect of the cult, careful calculation went into the selection and distribution of the photographic images of the Duce, with Mussolini personally deciding which pictures of him could be published. Among the most popular were those that featured him as "the first sportsman of Italy," a man in constant motion, fencing, swimming, skiing, on horseback or else riding motorcycles, driving sports cars, and flying airplanes. Such images highlighted Mussolini's youthful vitality, virility, and courage as well as his domination of the world of modern technology and speed. Another popular genre of the Duce pictures depicted him as a hardworking common man draining the swamps with a pick and shovel or else as a bare-chested harvester working in the fields alongside the peasants. Not only did these images link Mussolini to the manly virtues of productive work and the laboring classes, but they also played on his status as a sex symbol to millions of Italian women, who sent him a constant stream of love letters and treated him like a movie star. Later in the 1930s, the official poses increasingly projected a more intimidating image of the Duce as a leader with superhuman qualities and powers. To convey his lofty eminence and distance from ordinary people, his profile was featured in these pictures. He also wore a military uniform, combined with a steel helmet and shaved head, that emphasized his granite-like jaw and warlike demeanor.

By the late 1930s, the deification of Mussolini had taken on a life of its own. His birthplace in Predappio became a popular site for pilgrimages by millions of Italians; his "relics" became objects of veneration, and his picture was carried in local processions as if he were a patron saint. Stories even circulated regarding the Duce's miraculous powers. After a visit to Sicily in the early 1920s, for instance, rumors surfaced that Mussolini's mere presence had halted the flow of lava from Mt. Etna, thereby saving an entire village from destruction. On other occasions, his appeal had a decidedly less spiritual quality. When he went swimming at the beach, groups of screaming women would mob him, while men imitated his style and personal mannerisms. Predictably, private entrepreneurs cashed in on Mussolini's status as a celebrity by marketing products that made use of his image. His devoted fans could find everything from perfumed soap bars in the shape of the Duce to baby food advertisements and swimsuits that reproduced his picture.

The Fascist authorities and antifascists seemed to agree that the cult of the Duce represented the most popular and successful component of the regime. Government officials frequently noted the presence of an enthusiastic popular belief in Mussolini but warned that the cult was growing at the expense of the Fascist party, which met with popular indifference and cynicism because of its inefficiency and emphasis on rigid conformity. In fact, the declining popularity of the party actually reinforced the cult of the Duce as people concentrated their hopes for the future in the leadership of Mussolini. One police report captured this situation in 1932: "The mood of the people virtually everywhere is shifting more and more in favor of the Duce and [against] Fascism, whose image is shaped by local feuds and the less than exemplary behavior of party officials."

The views of the police found a clear echo in the writings of antifascists. The journalist Herbert L. Matthews, a harsh critic of fascism, conceded that in these years Mussolini enjoyed "an enormous popular consensus, tribute that was paid more to him personally than to the regime."

As time progressed, the cult enjoyed its strongest following among middle- and lower-middle-class Italians as well as among those rural folks who lacked strong secular political traditions. When protest demonstrations erupted against local landowners and officials in the countryside in the 1930s, the demonstrators reportedly marched to the chant of "Long live Mussolini." The cult had its greatest impact on the younger generation of Italians who had grown up under fascism. After a visit by Mussolini to her school, one student's diary entry described the experience in typically glowing terms:

> Sunday, 1 November, I came to school . . . because the Duce was coming . . . and we were all anxious to see him . . . . I was happy to see the Duce so near to me . . . . When the Duce got back in the car to leave us, sadly we waved goodbye though we were happy to have had him near us. It was only then we noticed the Duce had been attended by several officials but we had only had eyes for Him. This unforgettable day will live forever in our hearts.

Nor did the appeal of the Duce seem to be limited to young people from the middle classes or rural villages. Antifascist emigres frequently voiced their concern about the susceptibility of younger workers to the allures of Duce worship.

The first half of the 1930s also marked the high point of Mussolini's prestige and popularity abroad. The achievements of his regime, as trumpeted by Fascist propagandists, convinced at least some of the outside world during these years that the Duce had accomplished great things in Italy. Predictably, conservative politicians elsewhere praised him as man who had rescued his country from the menace of communist revolution and restored order and stability. Prominent British Tories like Winston Churchill, for example, portrayed him as "a great man" and publicly expressed their admiration for him. In a similar vein, the new German ambassador to Rome in 1933 gave a very positive assessment of the Duce: "He handled people like a man who was accustomed to having his orders obeyed, but displayed immense charm and did not give the impression of a revolutionary. Hitler always had a slight air of uncertainty, whereas Mussolini was calm, dignified, and appeared the complete master of whatever subject was being discussed." Authoritarian conservative leaders in Austria, Hungary, and Spain echoed these sentiments, looking to the Duce as their role model and political mentor in these years, while new Fascist groups in France and England openly emulated the style and methods of his movement.

Positive assessments of Mussolini were not limited to the conservative political camp or the European continent. In the early 1930s, British liberals and Labour party leaders spoke favorably about his public works projects. Mahatma Gandhi, the leader of the Indian independence movement, referred to him as the savior of the new Italy after their meeting in 1931, while the Chinese nationalist Chiang Kai Shek declared himself a great admirer of Mussolini. Even the liberal Democratic U.S. president, Franklin Delano Roosevelt, once described the Duce as "a true gentleman" and conceded that he was "deeply impressed by all that [Mussolini] has accomplished and by his proven effort to renew Italy . . . ." The American public, on the whole, appeared to have been interested in the Duce as a celebrity figure in the early 1930s, thanks to his reputation as a sportsman, self-made man, and virile lady's man.

A variety of circumstances contributed to Mussolini's international fame and prestige. The Duce's public persona was tailor-made for the popular tabloid press abroad, which fed their readership a steady diet of human interest stories about his sporting activities, love affairs, and even his dietary practices. More importantly, with much of the world in the early 1930s plunged into a deep economic depression that left most of the western democracies in crisis, the Duce and fascism appeared to offer a "third way" between liberal capitalism and soviet communism, a model of authority, decisiveness, and innovative policies needed to remedy the situation. As the American business weekly *Fortune* proclaimed in May 1932, "Mussolini remains solid. He displays . . . the virtue of strength and of a centralized government that acts quickly and without opposition for the benefit of the entire nation."

The reputation of the Duce also benefited from a very effective Fascist propaganda campaign of newsletters, films, and recorded speeches abroad, especially in the large Italian emigrant communities, that highlighted the regime's achievements and obscured its failures and shortcomings. At the same time, Mussolini and his press spokesmen succeeded, for the most part, in getting foreign journalists to transmit the official views of the regime in their papers. News stories coming out of Italy during the first half of the 1930s tended to focus on the efficiency of the train service, the draining of the swamps, the urban renewal of Rome, and the accomplishments of Italian athletes and adventurers. Even in the British and American print media, the antidemocratic and repressive aspects of Italian fascism received little or no attention in these years.

Despite a public image of the Duce as an international celebrity and superhero to the Italian people, Mussolini, who celebrated his fiftieth birthday in 1933, began to display physical changes that belied his image of perpetual youth, virility, and dynamism. Although the official rhetoric claimed that the Duce continued to highlight his "bronzed physique" and "rippling muscles," Mussolini's body had become noticeably chubbier, while his hairline had sharply receded and his hair was turning gray by the early 1930s. As early as 1925, Mussolini began to experience serious health problems. In the immediate aftermath of the Matteotti crisis, he suffered painful stomach cramps, vomited blood, and had to withdraw from the public for several weeks in February and March of that year. Diagnosed as having a bleeding peptic ulcer, he shifted to a vegetarian diet and gave up both alcohol and coffee, but the ulcer remained a recurring problem in the ensuing years.

By the early 1930s, Mussolini also began to display classic symptoms of a midlife crisis. The year he turned 50, Mussolini became involved with a much younger woman. The timing suggests that he did so to find a second youth and to demonstrate to himself and others that he had lost none of his virility and sexual appeal. His new mistress, Clara Petacci, was 19 in 1933—two years younger than the Duce's daughter, Edda—when the couple first became involved in a relationship that would continue for the rest of their lives.

The same years also witnessed important psychological changes in Mussolini. Even at the peak of his public fame and popularity as the Duce, his pessimism and cynicism about human nature became much more pronounced. From the outset, Mussolini was obsessed with making all political decisions himself because of his profound lack of confidence in other people's loyalty, reliability, and competence. To make matters worse, the premature death of his younger brother Arnaldo from a heart attack in 1931 deprived him of the only person whom he had ever trusted completely and greatly increased his sense of isolation. As he told one visitor the following year, "A chief cannot have equals. Nor friends. The humble solace gained from exchanging confidences is denied him. He cannot open his heart. Never." The loss of his brother clearly accentuated his distrust of others, including his oldest and closest collaborators. He was increasingly prone to view the most able Fascist leaders as potential rivals. As a result, he tended to transfer them away from positions of power and prominence, which he then either personally occupied or filled with lesser men. His distrust also became evident in many of the rituals of the regime that seemed designed to institutionalize his status as a man alone. By the early 1930s, Mussolini no longer socialized with or exchanged house visits with the families of other Fascist ministers. The transfer of his office after 1929 to the *Sala del Mappamondo* in central Rome reinforced this sense of separation. The vast *Sala* served to awe and intimidate visitors, who had to walk nearly twenty yards across a marble floor from the entrance to reach the Duce's desk.

By the second half of the 1930s, the enormous pressures of maintaining the facade of the all-knowing Duce began to take their toll on Mussolini, who complained that he had become "a prisoner . . . of others, of events, of hopes, of illusions." The preeminent political position he had achieved in Italy represented little more than "a gilded prison." He was well aware of the contrast between image and reality as he confessed in 1938: "I must often think what I do not say, and say what I do not think. Yes, there is a real gap between the two Mussolinis. Sometimes it is profound and terrible. Perhaps, one day, one of the two will beg an armistice, break his word and submit. I still don't know which one." These words reflected his awareness that, despite the claims of Fascist propaganda, he had made little headway in bringing about any fundamental transformation of Italian society and culture. With all his seemingly monumental institutional power and charismatic authority, Mussolini still had to contend with a number of deeply entrenched institutions, social groups, and collective attitudes and practices that limited both his freedom of action and his ability to reshape his country as he pleased.

V I

The Limits of Personal Power

1925–1938

Karl Marx, the founding father of modern socialism, once observed that "men make their own history, but they do not make it just as they please; they do not make it under circumstances chosen by themselves, but under circumstances directly encountered, given and transmitted from the past." In many respects, the evolution of Mussolini's dictatorship offers a striking confirmation of Marx's observation. Despite his virtual monopoly of institutional authority and his undeniable personal charisma, the Duce ultimately remained a prisoner of the historical circumstances and political compromises that had shaped his path to power in Italy. The Great War and the Russian Revolution largely determined who would be Mussolini's enemies and friends, thereby leaving an indelible mark on fascism. His Black Shirts emerged from political obscurity to national political prominence in 1920 thanks largely to their violent campaign against the Socialist party and its network of working-class organizations. The counterrevolutionary thrust of this campaign drew Mussolini into a marriage of convenience with older conservative institutions and wealthy propertied interests who felt threatened by the revolutionary left and thus benefited from fascism's destruction of the socialist labor movement.

The political consequences of the Great War in Italy further accentuated Mussolini's dependence on his respectable allies. Unlike in Germany, where military defeat led to the destruction of the old monarchical order, in Italy the war had weakened the governmental system but left intact an entrenched conservative establishment that included the monarchy, an army hierarchy, the Catholic church, and propertied notables. The survival of the old parliamentary order limited in turn the political space available to Mussolini and his movement. As a result, the Fascist party in Italy never achieved the electoral successes of the Nazis in Germany. In fact, the Fascists controlled only 35 of the 535 seats in the Chamber of Deputies before 1924. Under these circumstances, the Duce's political ambitions required that he and his party pursue two policies to hold on to power: first, to align themselves with conservative and nationalist parties and, second, to win the trust and support of the established institutions. Well before the March on Rome, he began to adopt these policies, abandoning the last vestiges of his old radicalism by embracing the cause of order, accepting the monarchy, and courting the favor of the Catholic hierarchy.

Mussolini's compromises with elements of the old establishment and wealthy propertied groups were critical to his political survival and then to the consolidation of his dictatorship. Beginning in the winter of 1920–1921, the dramatic expansion of the Fascist movement as a violent antisocialist force in the northern Italian countryside came about largely as the product of a merger between the *fasci* and the landowners' organizations that enjoyed the backing of local police and state officials. Two years later, the tacit support of the monarchy, the army, the Catholic church, and powerful business interests paved the way for Mussolini's semi-legal accession to the prime minister's office in October 1922. More importantly, the Fascist leader's ability to weather the storms unleashed by the murder of Matteotti depended on the tolerance shown by the king, the army, the Vatican, and influential industrial and banking leaders. Victor Emanuel III played an especially decisive role in the survival of fascism in 1924 by refusing to abdicate or demand the Duce's resignation. Likewise, the king played a quiet but important role in the years after 1925, dutifully signing all the laws that dismantled the constitutional liberal state and ushered in Mussolini's dictatorship.

The support of the king, the Vatican, and the Italian military came at a high price, however. The Fascist regime rested upon a set of compromises with these institutions that imposed important limitations both on Mussolini's freedom of action and on his totalitarian and modernizing ambitions. Whatever his intentions may have been, the Duce never managed to escape the consequences of these compromises with his establishment allies. As a result, the monarchy, the Catholic church, and the business elite continued to enjoy a significant degree of independence under the dictatorship. In this respect, the Fascist state in Italy differed profoundly from the Nazi regime that emerged in Germany after 1932. Unlike Hitler, Mussolini never succeeded in eliminating alternative centers of power or the political procedures that limited his authority and the totalitarian pretensions of his regime.

The monarchy remained the most important autonomous center of power after 1925. As the royal prime minister, the Duce shared political responsibilities with King Victor Emanuel III in a system of joint rule. He maintained formally correct relations with the short, homely, and timid monarch, but as Mussolini aptly put it, "the two shared a bedroom, but without a double bed in it." Victor Emanuel lacked the Duce's highly marketable charisma, and he displayed little inclination to challenge Mussolini's leadership or advance a competing political agenda of his own. Still, he remained the official head of state and "first soldier" of Italy, who had to be consulted on matters of war and possessed the legal authority to remove members of government from office. As a consequence, the officer corps and influential groups of old notables continued to give their principal loyalties to the throne rather than to the Duce. Moreover, the king used his position to prevent any attempt by Mussolini to transform or "fascistize" institutions like the Senate and the army, which Victor Emanuel deemed central to the monarchy's prestige and authority.

The king's protection meant that the Italian army enjoyed relative autonomy throughout the Fascist era. In the wake of the Great War, the armed forces confronted a number of organizational problems that needed to be addressed: too many officers, too few soldiers, outdated structures, and insufficient material reserves. However, the general staff, supported by the king, opposed as threats to their entrenched positions efforts by Mussolini's reform-minded minister of war, Antonino De Giorgio, to modernize the armed forces and increase their efficiency in 1924–1925. Once the Matteotti crisis erupted, Mussolini became reluctant to challenge the officer corps and abandoned any serious attempt to intervene in military affairs or impose an explicitly Fascist character on the army. The appointment in 1925 of the pro-monarchist Field Marshall Pietro Badoglio as chief of the general staff, a post that he kept until 1940, guaranteed the perpetuation of a pre-fascist status quo within the armed forces. Military leaders dutifully obeyed the orders of Mussolini and his regime, but their principal allegiances continued to lie with the monarchy and old institutions rather than with fascism. The Duce, for his part, was forced to rely on corruption and personal contacts to counterbalance the influence of the king within the officer corps. The resulting situation had profound long-term consequences for Mussolini and fascism, since it allowed the Italian army to avoid addressing serious shortcomings in armament, doctrine, organization, training, and leadership that persisted throughout the 1930s and into the Second World War.

Mussolini's skepticism and lack of confidence in the loyalty and abilities of his party stalwarts further increased his dependence on the old institutions. Distrust of his Fascist collaborators led the Duce to prefer a dictatorship based on hierarchy and order rather than on dynamism and action. His reluctance to give the party a prominent role in the construction of the regime and his reliance instead on the preexisting state bureaucracy wound up limiting his ability to translate his plans into practice. While professional bureaucrats possessed greater experience and technical expertise than their black-shirted counterparts, a majority of them were at best pragmatic converts to the cause. For the most part, these "fascist non-believers" favored a strong state but had little enthusiasm for any radical, activist agenda. In contrast to the fanatical Nazis who staffed the party-state in Germany, Italian officials displayed a traditional, pre-fascist mentality that inevitably affected the manner in which they executed their duties and responsibilities. When Mussolini's programs and policies diverged too sharply from familiar institutional norms and procedures, they encountered a stubborn, if passive, resistance within the ranks of the bureaucracy that limited or sabotaged their effectiveness.

The Duce faced institutional challenges to his power not only from the monarchy, army, and bureaucracy, but also from the Roman Catholic hierarchy. The church had long enjoyed a unique position and status on the Italian peninsula, where the overwhelming majority of the population was Catholic. For centuries the city of Rome had served both as the spiritual home of the church and the capital of a secular state in central Italy ruled over by the Pope. When the peninsula was unified in 1870, the papacy lost its power over the territorial state and retreated into "internal exile." Pope Pius IX and his successors refused to recognize the existence of the new nation and called on all Catholics to not participate in Italian political life. These policies ushered in a half-century of mutual hostility in church-state relations. Above all, the standoff undermined the efforts of Italy's governing class to forge a unified and cohesive nation by depriving it of the support of devout Catholics. When Mussolini came to power in 1922, there was still no formal reconciliation between church and state.

The Duce and the regime's propagandists certainly recognized the powerful emotional hold of Catholic ideology and cultural traditions on millions of Italians, especially in the countryside and small towns. Indeed, they paid homage to the prominent place of religion in Italian popular culture in their own spectacles and rituals, which appropriated recognizably Catholic practices, images, and language in an attempt to construct a much broader national political community. In their carefully orchestrated campaign to exalt the charisma of the dictator, for example, they surrounded him with an aura of religiosity. He appeared not simply as a greater leader, but as "our divine Duce," a "sublime redeemer," and the "man sent by God to Italy."

In the spring of 1920, Mussolini publicly recognized the legitimate authority of the Vatican and called for a merging of Catholicism with the nation. His courtship of the church intensified after the accession in 1922 of Pope Pius XI, who shared the Fascist leader's impatience with democratic procedures and his virulent anticommunism. Once in office, Mussolini further curried the favor of the Vatican in 1923 and 1924 by reintroducing the crucifix and catechism into state schools, exempting the clergy from taxation, providing aid to Catholic banks, and outlawing the Free Masons, an anti-clerical international secret society. The Duce's appeasement of the church even extended into his private life; he and Rachele were remarried in a Catholic ceremony and had their children baptized in the church. These concessions were more than simply tactical moves on his part. They also reflected his awareness that the two sides shared common socialist and democratic enemies as well as a common concern for discipline, authority, and hierarchy.

Mussolini's courtship of the Catholic hierarchy paid off not only in the vital support the Vatican gave him during the Matteotti crisis. It also led to a new willingness on the part of Pius XI to reach a formal understanding with the regime on the question of church-state relations in Italy after 1925. With the dictatorship in place, formal negotiations for a treaty between the Fascist regime and the papacy began in 1926 and continued for another three years. Under Mussolini's direct supervision, the two sides worked on an agreement to compensate the church for the loss of its old territories and to resolve differences over Fascist educational policies and the role of Catholic youth groups. The resulting settlement, the Lateran Accords, which the regime officially announced in February 1929, involved three agreements: a financial settlement for the church, a treaty granting papal sovereignty over Vatican City in Rome in return for Catholic recognition of the Italian state, and a detailed concordat defining the status of Catholicism in Fascist Italy.

The Duce reaped enormous immediate benefits from the reconciliation he had orchestrated with the Catholic church. Both at home and abroad, public opinion greeted the concordat and treaty as a tremendous political success and personal triumph for the Fascist dictator, who had accomplished something that had eluded all of his predecessors. Within Italy, Pius XI praised Mussolini as the "man whom providence has sent us," while the vast majority of Catholics enthusiastically rallied to the regime and embraced the cult of the Duce. Even his detractors conceded that Mussolini's reconciliation with the church marked "the highest point of his parabola" as the charismatic leader of Italy. At the political level, the Fascist leader also received the backing of the church for a number of his domestic and foreign policy initiatives. During the 1930s, Catholic authorities embraced the regime's demographic, economic, and expansionist foreign policies. Finally, the Lateran Accords gave a dramatic boost to the Duce's international prestige and stature as a "great and daring" statesman, especially among Catholic forces in other countries, who openly celebrated the dictator as an "intellectual giant" and trumpeted the achievements of his regime in their newspapers and magazines.

In the years that followed, however, Mussolini discovered that the benefits of his compromise with the most powerful conservative institution in Italy came at a stiff price. From the outset, the concordat limited fascism's totalitarian pretensions by expanding the Vatican's legal authority in a variety of areas, including those of marriage, family, religious instruction, and self-government. More importantly, the Lateran Accords clearly belied the Duce's claims to total personal power, since they sanctioned the presence of the papacy as a separate center of doctrine and propaganda in Italy, acting independently of the Fascist regime. Much to Mussolini's chagrin, church authorities steadfastly refused to merge with the regime or support its policies unconditionally. On the contrary, the Vatican took advantage of its new legal rights to try to expand its own organizational presence and influence in Italian social life. The rapid growth of clerical organizations and activities after 1929 finally led to a violent crackdown by the regime in 1931 that restricted the freedom and activities of the leading association, Catholic Action, and its youth affiliates. Nonetheless, Catholic Action weathered the crackdown of that year to remain the only major organizational network to survive outside the structures of the Fascist state. As such, it helped to limit the impact of Fascist youth policies and to perpetuate a Catholic identity in Italian life. At the same time, church authorities continued to exert their independence in matters of doctrine and policy by intervening aggressively on political and educational issues near and dear to their hearts. Indeed, they publicly condemned those policies of the regime that deviated from papal teachings, openly challenging the Duce's totalitarian aspirations.

Mussolini's freedom of action was limited not only by the relative political autonomy of the monarchy, church, and army, but also by the social and economic elites who subsidized and promoted fascism's rise to power. In the 1920s, Mussolini engaged in a variety of compromises with industrial and agrarian elites against the Italian left and the organized labor movement. These compromises emerged first and most strikingly in the countryside, where provincial Fascists forged an alliance with landowners and big commercial farmers to launch a joint assault on the Socialist municipal administrations, cooperatives, and labor unions. The ensuing violence and coercion of the squads destroyed the "red" leagues of farm workers that had threatened agrarian profits, managerial prerogatives, and property rights after the Great War. Moreover, the Fascists replaced the old unions with their own labor organizations, which were considerably more accommodating to the landowners. The Fascist labor syndicates offered landowners and commercial farmers various benefits. The syndicates controlled labor discontent by force and left employers relatively free to dictate the terms of employment to workers in agriculture. This bias toward wealthy landed interests did not change with the creation of the dictatorship after 1925. Mussolini's regime developed a set of institutional arrangements that consistently favored his entrenched allies, the big landowners and commercial farmers, over those social groups that had once supported his socialist adversaries.

While the government generally subordinated the interests of agriculture to those of industry in the 1930s, it provided wealthy agrarian capitalists with a range of mechanisms to protect their profits and escape the worst effects of the Great Depression. First, the absence of an independent labor movement and the presence of a powerful police state apparatus allowed the big growers to respond to falling farm prices by slashing their workers' wages or by returning to sharecropping arrangements that shifted more of the expenses and risks to the peasant laborers. Likewise, landowners succeeded in having farm workers excluded from the regime's social welfare system and unemployment benefits. The same agricultural interests, especially in the northern plains, also became the chief beneficiaries of Fascist policies of grain protection and projects of land reclamation to drain the swamps that greatly strengthened their position as direct producers and financial intermediaries in the countryside. They sat on the boards of the reclamation consortia and banks, using the authority of the state and public funds to advance their private interests. Finally, the capitalist farmers profited directly from the privileged treatment the Fascists accorded to producers of the crops that were the mainstays of commercial agriculture. The regime established protective tariffs and export subsidies for sugar beets, hemp, and rice that raised the prices of these commercial crops at home while lowering them in foreign markets. The Fascists also promoted policies of cartelization, rationalization, and production controls to bolster the profits of the commercial farmers. In the countryside, the real losers in this process of advancement were the peasant laborers, who suffered from increased exploitation, rising underemployment, and a diminished standard of living.

Industrialists, for their part, enjoyed even greater autonomy and influence than their agricultural counterparts within the institutional structures developed by Mussolini and the Fascists after 1924. From the outset, Italy's fragile financial status in the 1920s increased the leverage of big business in its dealings with the government. Much like his predecessors, Mussolini faced an enormous wartime debt and perennial balance-of-payments deficits. Any attempt to address these problems necessitated cooperation from the industrial and financial leaders of Turin and Milan. The economic elite exploited their clout to win major concessions from Mussolini in exchange for their support. In fact, the principal lobbying body for Italian business interests, the Confederation of Italian Industry, or Confindustria, managed to carve out a remarkably independent position of power within the ostensibly monolithic regime, a position that enabled it to oppose policies that limited entrepreneurial freedom. In this fashion, strategic industrial groups did considerably more than simply preserve most of their old prerogatives. They also succeeded in increasing their access to the government and thereby expanding their own private power at the expense of workers and the regime's social welfare initiatives.

The rewards industrialists received from the Fascists' antisocialist campaign and their support of Mussolini during the March on Rome in 1922 and the Matteotti crisis of 1924 came with the Vidoni Palace Agreement of October 1925 and the syndical law, governing the structure of labor-management relations, the following year. The first, an agreement between Confindustria and Fascist labor leaders, provided immediate benefits to industrial employers with relatively few concessions on their part. Above all, it greatly strengthened the authority of management within the workplace by excluding non-fascist unions from collective bargaining and by eliminating the Socialist-dominated workers' factory councils. Moreover, management won these concessions without giving up its independence to the government and the Fascist party. While the industrialists had to accept the principle of compulsory arbitration with the Fascist labor syndicates, they gained the right to settle disputes outside the courts and avoided having to grant immediate wage hikes.

Confindustria also prevailed in the organization of labor-management relations. The new syndical law of 1926 stipulated the creation of twelve national syndicates or corporations, covering all the major sectors of the economy, with workers and employers organized in separate but collaborative bodies. Proponents of Fascist "corporatism" envisioned a system in which spokesmen for labor and management would work together to plan and coordinate economic production within each sector, but industrial leaders effectively sabotaged this vision. Although all the syndicates theoretically enjoyed equal standing, Confindustria emerged as the most powerful, combining the freedom of a private association with the public power of a state agency. The law designated Confindustria as the official and exclusive representative of all industrial employers in their relations with labor and the government. As such, it acquired the legal authority of a public agency, firmly entrenched in the institutional system of the dictatorship with a permanent seat on the Fascist Grand Council and governmental planning bodies. At the same time, the leaders of Confindustria preserved their administrative autonomy and continued to act as a pressure group on behalf of private business interests, while labor representatives were appointed by the government and had little connection to the rank and file. Confindustria's dual role made it strong enough to neutralize any major innovation and to manipulate Fascist economic and social policies in ways that protected the profit margins of industrialists. Yet these tangible benefits did not translate into enthusiastic and unqualified support for Mussolini and fascism. As a frustrated Duce conceded, the industrialists gave at best only "a purely formal adherence to the regime."

The consequences of these arrangements for industrialists, workers, and the regime became strikingly evident with the arrival of the Great Depression in the 1930s. Much as elsewhere in Europe and in the United State, prices on the Italian stock market plummeted, the banking system was shaken, production and exports were both down, and unemployment had soared by the middle of the decade. For their part, hard-pressed industrialists received public financial assistance with surprisingly little government regulation and oversight. In January 1933, the regime created a new state agency, the Istituto per la Ricostruzione Industriale (Institute for Industrial Reconstruction), or IRI, to rescue hard-pressed industrial firms. In the following years IRI's subsidies and bailouts freed private business groups from their unprofitable or failing enterprises and enabled them to focus on more lucrative investments. The bigger industrial firms also profited from government-sponsored cartels that gave them a virtual free hand to coordinate the distribution of raw materials, production quotas, and pricing and marketing policies in their sectors.

The privileged position of these influential economic groups enabled them to transfer most of the material sacrifices of the Great Depression onto the laboring classes, a circumstance with profound consequences for Mussolini's aspirations to fascistize Italian society. The Duce had little room for maneuver, since he was already committed politically and institutionally to his wealthy allies. Deprived of independent representation and the right to strike, Italian workers had no effective means of protecting their jobs, working conditions, and wage levels. Not surprisingly, in the years after 1929 the economic crisis hit factory workers especially hard. Their incomes plummeted while their rates of unemployment and underemployment soared. Indeed, in the early 1930s the ranks of the jobless quadrupled. The same period also witnessed Fascist labor syndicates agreeing to a series of across-the-board wage cuts for blue-collar workers. Mussolini's much-touted social welfare system did little to compensate labor because he was reluctant to pressure employers on questions of wages and worker incomes. The regime's overly ambitious and poorly coordinated welfare bureaucracy lacked both the material resources and the organizational efficiency to provide efficient service or adequate levels of economic assistance. To make matters worse, the distribution of welfare, pensions, and social insurance benefits favored white-collar employees—the backbone of the regime—over industrial workers. Data on food consumption by Italians during the 1930s eloquently testify to the human costs of Fascism's social biases. Consumption of meat, sugar, fats, and carbohydrates all dropped in these years, along with the daily caloric intake of the population.

The failure of Mussolini's regime to improve the standard of living for its people undermined his efforts to win over the hearts and minds of Italy's working masses. The agencies of his police state could impose discipline and passive submission on the workers, but Mussolini could not generate much in the way of enthusiasm or voluntary support for the Fascist system. The Duce's carefully nurtured charisma continued throughout the 1930s to assure him a strong mass following, but his personal magnetism did not translate into a larger popular identification with a regime that rewarded the strong and punished the weak. Protesting economic conditions in 1930, demonstrators in the city of Turin captured the limits of the cult of the Duce with their slogan, "Long live the Duce! But we want to eat!"

Even if he had not compromised with the old institutions and pre-fascist elites, Mussolini still would have had to contend with the realities of inter-war Italy, a relatively poor and unevenly developed country whose underlying socioeconomic and cultural structures imposed limits on his ability to reshape the Italian people as he pleased. The Duce could do little about the country's shortages of fertile land, vital energy resources, and venture capital or its natural barriers to rapid internal transportation and communications. Even in the late 1930s, Italy still lacked an integrated electricity system and a fully developed network of modern mass communications. Access to telephones and radios remained limited. In 1939, in a population of 42.9 million people, there were only 600,000 privately owned telephones and 806,000 radios. Moreover, aggregate statistics on the Italian economy concealed enormous regional imbalances in industrial development, wealth, and consumption. The north, with its major urban centers of Milan, Turin, and Genoa, accounted for 19 percent of the country's land surface and a quarter of its population, but contributed 40 percent of the national income.

Although some industrial development did take place in the Fascist era, especially in the more technologically advanced sectors, a substantial gap persisted between Italy and the other industrialized countries of Europe and the west. By the late 1930s, Italy ranked well behind the United States, England, Russia, Germany, France, and Japan in terms of national income, manufacturing, and (with the exception of France) population. Its national income was less than half that of France's, a third of Germany's, and a quarter of England's. In 1938, the country ranked eighteenth among twenty European states in its people's caloric intake. On the eve of World War II, British manufacturers built more than six times as many tanks, buses, and automobiles and more than triple the number of railroad locomotives as their Italian counterparts, while the French produced three times as much steel.

In the absence of sustained economic growth and modernization, the majority of Mussolini's people continued to live in a comparatively traditional and loosely integrated society. In 1921, 56 percent of the Italian people earned their livelihoods in agriculture; a third of them could neither read nor write, and many more were semiliterate. Significantly, these conditions had not changed greatly after nearly 15 years of dictatorship. On the eve of World War II, nearly half of the population still worked in the agricultural sector, while illiteracy rates remained high in the countryside, especially in southern Italy. Mussolini's regime possessed none of the social and financial resources of Nazi Germany, for instance, which inherited a rich tradition of organizational life and enjoyed comparatively high levels of mass consumption and employment. In the case of Italy, poor communications, poverty, illiteracy, and weak traditions of voluntary organization meant that large segments of the population continued to live in isolation from the outside world throughout the inter-war period. As Achille Starace, the head of the Fascist party, lamented in 1938, Italian peasants "when not simply apathetic or recalcitrant, have been little inclined toward any form of organized activity."

Persistent social and economic stagnation limited popular participation in the official initiatives of the regime like the leisure-time organizations, hampering the penetration of such Fascist values as physical fitness, national solidarity, and martial discipline into the larger society. The growing impoverishment of Italy's working classes during the Great Depression reduced purchasing power and made workers less able to participate in fascism's organized activities. Hardship and deprivation also shaped how participants experienced these pastimes. Recalling the 1930s in the southern city of Potenza, one local man observed:

> Notwithstanding all the big talk about "faith" in Fascist Italy, in the imperial destiny of the nation, and in the "Duce," what I saw every day was the wretched spectacle of a bunch of humble people who liked the quiet life adapting themselves to living from day to day without "making waves." They did this by donning the Fascist boots and uniform with no other preoccupation than keeping their position or acquiring some privilege that would allow them to live in a less sordid way . . .

The relative poverty of the country meant that Mussolini's government lacked the revenues to construct the facilities, provide the equipment, and subsidize adequately the ambitious social programs and activities intended to assimilate its followers into a new national community. Many of the most promising initiatives of the Fascist leisure-time organizations, for instance, remained underfunded and unevenly distributed between cities and rural areas and between north and south.

At the same time, the absence of a strong system of mass education, a genuine common language, and a popular print culture frustrated Mussolini's attempts to replace established cultural norms and identities with those of the new "Fascist Man." Despite the constant propaganda and mass spectacles of the regime, most people in the countryside and small towns of Italy continued in the 1930s to identify with an older set of values, customs, and practices associated with family, hometown, and religion. The Catholic church's deep roots and reassuring rituals were formidable obstacles to the diffusion of Fascist values among the faithful. The clergy continued to exercise a stronger influence than the government on popular beliefs and behavior in many areas of the country. Even fascism's facade of efficiency and military discipline often masked older methods of informal deal-making and personal understandings that still shaped the processes of decision-making. In fact, the institutions of the totalitarian regime proved no less vulnerable than their liberal predecessors to manipulation by patron-client networks and family connections in the distribution of public jobs, promotions, and contracts. Especially in southern Italy, local Fascist leaders relied on the same old strategies, seeking the personal intervention of the Duce against their enemies and using their positions to reward their loyal clients within the rapidly expanding state bureaucracy.

If traditional institutions and mentalities limited the ideological penetration of fascism in the Italian countryside, Mussolini's efforts to construct a tougher and more disciplined citizenry faced a formidable challenge from American models of consumer culture in the major cities. American popular culture, with its emphasis on glamorous new lifestyles and modes of self-expression through consumption, began to attract a following among middle-class urbanites and more affluent young people in inter-war Italy. Radio, movies, novels, department stores, and pulp magazines all exposed these groups to styles of courtship, fashion, and leisure that together offered them an alternative vision of "modern life" to that advanced by fascism. Even Mussolini's own daughter and a role model for upper-class young women, Edda Ciano, considered it chic to drink Coca-Cola.

The regime's spokesmen certainly recognized the insidious cultural threat posed by the United States and the American way of life. As one of them cautioned: "Today's enemy is unarmed. . . . He enters into your house via newspapers, photographs, and books that diffuse his mentality.

Look around you, Italians, and you'll see Americanism all around you." The films coming out of Hollywood, which accounted for 70 percent of the movies in circulation within the country, enjoyed an enormous appeal among Italian moviegoers, who clearly preferred them to their own country's movies in the 1930s. In 1938, for example, 40 Italian movies competed ineffectually with 200 films from the United States. Italian authorities decried the supposed cynicism and materialism of the American films, warning that the images they projected encouraged Italian men to reject virile Fascist ideals and instead walk around with "dead fish-eyes like Valentino" or "flashing a Ramon Navarro smile." Measures by the regime to reduce the influence of American cinema met with scant success; middle-class Italians continued to flock to the theaters to see Westerns and other B movies in the last years before the war.

Already in the mid-1930s, it was increasingly clear that the Duce's institutional authority and personal mass following were not producing any sweeping transformation of Italian society and culture. The tenacity of older norms and values, the abiding clout of established institutions and elites, and the allure of cultural models from abroad all combined to limit his ability to be "an iron-hard engineer of human souls" within Italy.

To make matters worse, troubled state finances, high unemployment, falling wages, and the lack of progress in constructing the corporative system made a mockery of fascism's image as a modernizing force for improving the lot of the common man. The gap between the exalted promises of his regime and its actual accomplishments provoked Mussolini's mounting frustration and anger. Predictably, he blamed the failings of fascism on the flawed character of the Italian people and the resistance of his conservative allies. As a result, the Duce turned to a policy of military expansionism abroad to break the domestic deadlock, revitalize his regime, and bolster its flagging prestige.

VII

Mussolini, the Warlord

1935–1938

During his first ten years in power, Mussolini's importance in the world rested on what he had done within the borders of his own country. When the Duce's foreign supporters and admirers praised him, it was usually for what they saw as his domestic accomplishments. They highlighted his elimination of the communist threat in his country, his restoration of order, discipline, and efficiency, and his seemingly innovative solutions to the problems posed by the Great Depression. Likewise, Mussolini's critics blamed him for the destruction of Italy's liberal democratic state, the repression of Italy's working-class movement, and the elimination of political freedom at home. From 1935 onward, the Duce achieved international notoriety for his foreign policies. He began to attract the attention of the world as the irresponsible and dangerous leader

Mussolini, the
Fascist warlord
of the 1930s

of a rogue state bent on expansion and the violent overthrow of the international status quo.

Mussolini had long cultivated an image as a man with rather bellicose views on international relations. Even in his role as a revolutionary socialist before 1914, he had portrayed all politics as a struggle for survival, dominated by rival elites and states who necessarily employed violence and war to achieve their objectives. After his break with the Socialists, he emphasized the idea that war was the best means of unifying and empowering the Italian people. Armed conflict, he asserted, would forge a new nation of fearless and disciplined warriors. During the last years of the Great War, he also began to espouse ultranationalist and imperialist ideas about Italy's place in Europe and the Mediterranean. After the war he openly attacked the international peace settlement at Versailles as a betrayal of "proletarian" Italy's national destiny by her rich western allies, France and England, who had refused to hand over the Austrian territories promised to her in 1915. Not surprisingly, he called for a sweeping revision of the territorial arrangements made at the Paris Peace Conference. Proclaiming that "imperialism is the eternal and imputable law of life," Mussolini advocated Italian expansion into the new neighboring states of southeastern Europe in the first years after the war.

Once Mussolini was in office, though, his government pursued a two-track foreign policy throughout the 1920s and into the early 1930s. On the one hand, Mussolini challenged the postwar status quo. He continued to make inflammatory statements about Italy's role as "a great power" and her need for *spazio vitale* (living space); he privately talked of war against France and Yugoslavia to gain the promised territories lost in the postwar peace accords. In 1923, he did more than talk, ordering his navy to seize the island of Corfu from Greece by force, as an "immediate and exemplary punishment" for the murders of Italian members of a Greco-Albanian border commission. During the ensuing years he held clandestine meetings with the German radical right and meddled in the domestic politics of Yugoslavia, subsidizing the activities of Croatian and Macedonian separatists as well as Muslim forces in Kosovo. All of these initiatives aspired to undermine and revise the Versailles international agreements.

On the other hand, Mussolini's official diplomatic corps pursued a relatively conventional foreign policy during the 1920s, one that maintained cooperation with the western democracies and friendly relations with Yugoslavia. His government quickly withdrew its forces from Corfu in 1923 in response to diplomatic pressure from England, France, and the League of Nations. Likewise, representatives of his regime dutifully carried out the responsibilities of Italy's membership in the League of Nations and took part in international efforts toward securing peace, including the Treaty of Locarno in 1925 and the Kellogg-Briand Pact of 1928. Despite the Duce's occasional tough talk and secret initiatives, his regime's foreign policy displayed little dynamism or strong ideological tendencies in these years. Generally, Mussolini left foreign affairs in the hands of professional diplomats who continued to pursue Italy's traditional goals of security in Europe and friendship with England and France. Such an approach kept his regime out of trouble, but it did little to increase the prestige of Fascist Italy in the world.

Both domestic and international circumstances dictated Mussolini's cautious and conventional foreign policies in the 1920s. Throughout most of the decade, his highest priority remained the consolidation of the Fascist regime and his personal power at home. Initially, the turbulent and unstable domestic situation in Italy and the Duce's need for the support of influential conservative interests encouraged him to avoid aggressive moves abroad. In the second half of the decade, he had to devote most of his time and energy to the construction of his new totalitarian state at the expense of any major initiative in foreign affairs.

The international situation in the 1920s also imposed its own constraints on the Duce's diplomatic freedom of action. While the Great War had eliminated Italy's principal antagonist, the Austro-Hungarian Empire, and opened up new opportunities for expansion into the Balkans, other circumstances were considerably less favorable to Mussolini's government. Imperial Germany's defeat in 1918 deprived Italy of her old counterweight to French power on the continent. To make matters worse, the Fascist regime could ill afford to antagonize England and the United States, since Italy's war debts and chronic balance of trade deficits made her dependent on their financial support. Moreover, England, the dominant sea power in the Mediterranean, displayed little sympathy for Italian imperial ambitions in a region vital to her own colonial interests. In any case, the relative weakness of Italy's industrial base seemed to preclude any massive program of rearmament necessary for an expansionist foreign policy.

Changing circumstances at home and abroad in the 1930s, however, created a new set of problems and opportunities that encouraged Mussolini to turn his attention to the arena of foreign affairs. On the one hand, the Duce firmly controlled the domestic front by the end of the 1920s. The antifascists had been routed; most of the key institutions of the totalitarian state were largely in place; and the Duce enjoyed mass support as well as the backing of Italy's established institutions. Mussolini had managed to assert his political control over the Ministry of Foreign Affairs by forcing many of the senior members of the professional diplomatic corps into retirement and replacing them with Fascist loyalists. On the other hand, the unchallenged political dominance

of fascism also gave the regime exclusive responsibility for the economic and social problems that
continued to beset Italy, especially with the arrival of the Great Depression. Despite its highly
publicized programs and institutional innovations, fascism had largely failed to carry out its
promised transformation of Italian society by the
mid-1930s. On the contrary, the regime still confronted enormous problems of mass unemployment, poverty, and stagnation in a country where
the people remained wedded to pre-fascist values,
customs, and practices.

In this difficult and discouraging domestic setting, the adoption of an aggressive, expansionist
foreign policy promised a number of benefits to
Mussolini and his regime. First of all, territorial
expansion represented a potential solution to
Italy's economic problems by reducing unemployment and providing industry with access to
vital raw materials and new markets. Overseas
military adventures could also serve to divert
popular attention away from the internal shortcomings of fascism's domestic campaigns. Under
the best of circumstances, such adventures would
shake the Italian people out of their lethargy and
parochialism, arousing in them a new sense of
patriotic pride and national solidarity. Foreign
triumphs offered the prospect not only of en-
hancing the personal prestige of the Duce, but

also of rekindling mass enthusiasm for a regime that had seemingly lost its momentum at home.

Drastic changes in the diplomatic situation in the early 1930s created additional incentives and opportunities for Mussolini to embrace a more aggressive stance in foreign affairs. The accession of Adolf Hitler to power in Germany, in particular, greatly altered the balance of power in Europe and the Duce's standing on the continent. From the outset, the emergence of the Nazi regime in 1933 destabilized the international order constructed at the end of the Great War. Hitler's stated intentions to overthrow the Treaty of Versailles, rearm his country, and expand Germany's presence in Central Europe undermined existing diplomatic arrangements and posed a new threat to collective security on the continent. For his part, Mussolini responded to developments in Germany with a contradictory mixture of sympathy, jealousy, fear, and resentment. The two men and their regimes clearly enjoyed strong ideological affinities. In particular, the Duce and Hitler shared a similar hostility to democracy and pacifism as well as contempt for the League of Nations and disarmament. On the other hand, Mussolini also recognized that the Nazi leader's ambitions in Central Europe and especially Austria threatened Italy's national interests on its northern borders and in the

Balkans. On a more personal level, the German dictator's seizure of power in Europe's largest and most powerful country stole the international spotlight away from the Duce, who suddenly found himself relegated to a secondary role on the European stage. Finally, Hitler deprived him of the status and influence he had enjoyed for over a decade as the leading exponent of fascism in the world.

At the same time, Hitler's disruption of the European status quo and the threat he posed to England and France presented immediate opportunities for Fascist Italy to realize its own imperial ambitions. By the mid-1930s, England and France became increasingly focused on the crisis in Europe created by Nazi Germany, a crisis that accentuated the importance of Italian cooperation in any new security arrangements. Efforts to reach a diplomatic settlement to achieve multilateral disarmament in 1934 ended in failure; in the same year Nazi Germany withdrew from the League of Nations. As a result, Mussolini saw an opportunity for a quick and easy military conquest on the African continent before Nazi Germany could make any decisive move in Central Europe, a conquest that would both display Italy's power and assert the Duce's own stature as a great military leader to be feared and respected in world politics.

Mussolini's designated target of opportunity was Ethiopia, an independent state in the horn of Africa and a member in good standing of the League of Nations. A variety of diplomatic and historical considerations dictated its selection. To begin with, Ethiopia was the only country in Africa whose conquest did not threaten the colonial interests of the other European powers. In fact, France and England long had recognized Italy's zone of influence in East Africa, where she had already established colonies in neighboring Eritrea, Somalia, and Libya before 1914. The conquest of Ethiopia thus offered Mussolini a link to Italy's older colonies, a commanding position on the Red Sea, and a base for further penetration in the region. Nor did the African country's poorly equipped army or its 11-plane air force pose a major threat to a highly mechanized Italian military. Such a campaign also could count on broad support at home, since it would settle an old score with the East African country dating back to the end of the nineteenth century. In 1896, the Ethiopians had inflicted a humiliating defeat on the Italians at the Battle of Adowa, ending the country's colonial initiatives there for two generations. For Fascists and other fervent nationalists, Adowa remained an unacceptable stain on the honor of the country that could be cleansed only by a resounding victory on the battlefield.

The Duce gambled that he could embark on a war in Ethiopia without damaging permanently Fascist Italy's standing in the international community or her relations with the other great powers. From the outset, he calculated that the French and English could hardly advance major objections to his invasion, since he was acting in Africa in much the same way as they had in the nineteenth century. In any case, the preoccupation of the two western democracies with the emerging Nazi threat in Europe, he assumed, would encourage them to acquiesce to his African adventure. Likewise, the refusal of the League of Nations to take concrete measures against Japan's invasion of Manchuria encouraged Mussolini to gamble that his invasion of Ethiopia would produce only token opposition from that international body.

Mussolini's war aims in Africa exposed his ruthlessness and brutality. He demanded from his military leaders nothing less than the total destruction of the Ethiopian army and the complete incorporation of the territory into Fascism's new "Roman Empire." Since his own prestige required that the victory be quick and decisive, he was prepared to employ any and all means of warfare. His regime's earlier campaign to crush colonial resistance in Libya had already demonstrated his willingness to enact policies that would be considered crimes against humanity and would qualify Mussolini as an international war criminal today. Between 1928 and 1933, he endorsed the use of poison gas against civilian targets and carried out a campaign of "ethnic cleansing" that forced from the interior a population of 100,000 Libyan men, women, and children. These refugees were put into concentration camps where more than half perished from hunger and disease by mid-1933. To achieve equally decisive results in Ethiopia, war preparations began in earnest during the first five months of 1935. When they were completed Mussolini had dispatched to Africa one of the largest colonial expeditions in history, a force numbering more than 400,000 troops and 100,000 civilian workers.

Such a massive troop buildup did not go unnoticed either in the other European capitals or at home. Under pressure from its own people, the British government refused to condone unprovoked and unilateral military aggression by Italy in Ethiopia because they considered this to be a violation of international peacekeeping agreements and a direct threat to the League of Nations. Despite a formal treaty between Italy and France in early 1935, the conservative government of Pierre Laval also wound up withholding any official approval of the invasion, if only out of a need to stand by her vital English ally. For its part, the League of Nations took a tougher stand than expected, promising to impose economic sanctions on the Italian regime in the event of war.

Initially, Mussolini's conservative domestic allies also had serious reservations about the impending invasion. King Victor Emanuel III and the old-line diplomats were alarmed by Nazi Germany's territorial ambitions within Europe and worried that the invasion of Ethiopia would fatally undermine Italy's friendship with England, the traditional foundation of her foreign policy. Elements of the armed forces also opposed the Duce's war plan because it weakened Italy's military presence in Europe, entailed daunting technical difficulties as a campaign thousands of miles from home, and reduced the autonomy of the army hierarchy. Finally, industrial and banking interests voiced concern about the financial impact of the war and the potential disruptions of economic sanctions.

In the face of these domestic and foreign challenges to his war plans, Mussolini displayed once again a combination of opportunism, energy, determination, and intuition. He steadfastly refused to back down or compromise in the months leading up to the invasion. On the home front, the Duce and his propagandists mobilized popular support for the war by portraying it both as a natural expression of Italy's great power status and as a civilizing mission among the primitive Africans. The Fascist press assured the Italian people that their country was not an aggressor, but rather the victim of the rich and decadent democracies of Western Europe bent on denying her rightful place as a great nation in the world. While Mussolini went through the motions of reassuring the English government of his continuing collaboration and friendship in Europe and the Mediterranean, he sabotaged efforts by the League of Nations and England to negotiate a peaceful settlement of the crisis.

The Duce was equally resolute in imposing his war plans on his nervous domestic allies, who, in any case, were already well disposed to the idea of a colony in Ethiopia. He and his closest advisers launched military preparations with a minimum amount of consultation from the monarchy, military, or industrial leaders. Despite his initial reservations, the king ended up supporting the invasion, fearful that any concerted effort to stop Mussolini might undermine the entire regime and provoke dangerous divisions within the armed forces. In a similar fashion, the other principal traditional institutions and groups put aside their concerns and rallied around the flag. While the Vatican maintained a position of official neutrality, the Italian bishops as well as the Catholic press and lay organizations openly supported the regime's "crusade" in Africa.

The war in Ethiopia and its immediate repercussions at home and abroad seemed to confirm the wisdom of the Duce's intuitions and tactics. On October 3, 1935, Mussolini launched his invasion of the African country without a formal declaration of war. Full-scale military operations began two months later after attempts at a negotiated settlement ended in failure. The huge Italian expeditionary force exploited its vast numerical and technological superiority as well as its complete domination of the skies to overwhelm the poorly organized and ill-equipped Ethiopian resistance. Much as in Libya five years earlier, Mussolini authorized his generals to employ "all means of war necessary, I say all, both from the air and on the ground," including bacterial agents, to ensure a quick and decisive victory. To terrorize the population into submission, the Italian forces indiscriminately bombed towns, roads, hospitals, and other civilian targets and made extensive use of poison gas. After a string of victories on the battlefield in the first months of 1936, the rapidly advancing Italian army captured the Ethiopian capital, Addis Ababa, on May 5. Four days later, the Duce, with the new "Emperor of Abyssinia," King Victor Emanuel

III at his side, proclaimed to an enthusiastic crowd of 200,000 people in Rome that "Italy finally has its empire . . . . It is a Fascist empire, an empire of peace, an empire of civilization and humanity."

The rather ineffectual response of the international community to the Italian invasion of Ethiopia seemed to confirm Mussolini's assumptions about the division and disarray of the western powers. On October 11, 1935, the League of Nations formally condemned Italy as an aggressor for its attack on a member state. Fifty-two countries agreed to apply economic sanctions against her that included an embargo on arms, munitions, loans, and credits. The actual embargo, however, had only a limited impact on Italy since it permitted the continued importation of oil and other primary resources essential to Mussolini's war effort. Moreover, four countries sympathetic to Fascist Italy—Austria, Hungary, Albania, and Paraguay—along with the non-member states, Germany, the United States, and Japan, rejected this limited boycott. Even the British government was reluctant to take a really tough stand against Mussolini. London dispatched a beefed-up naval fleet into the eastern Mediterranean in September 1935 but then refused to close off the Suez Canal to Italian shipping.

The League's economic sanctions had little immediate effect on the war, but they were very effective in rallying public opinion in Italy behind the Duce. Italians initially greeted the decision for war without much enthusiasm. On the whole, they shared elite concerns about the impact on the economy and Italy's international position in waging a war not in defense of the homeland, but of distant conquest. The embargo, however, provoked public anger and resentment that the regime quickly capitalized on to mobilize a popular patriotic reaction against the League of Nations and the English government. Under the auspices of Fascist authorities, Italians boycotted foreign imports and donated precious metals to the war effort in mass ceremonies throughout the country. As the risk of armed confrontation with the English faded and the nation's forces achieved a series of quick victories with few casualties, the majority of Italians were swept up in a wave of collective exaltation and enthusiasm for the war that reached its peak in the summer of 1936 with the occupation of Addis Ababa and the proclamation of the Italian empire in Africa.

In the short run, the Ethiopian War represented a tremendous personal triumph for Mussolini and marked the pinnacle of his popularity within Italy. As the leading Fascist philosopher,

Giovanni Gentile, proclaimed in May, the Duce had "not just founded empire in Ethiopia . . . . He has created a new Italy." Even prominent antifascists like Carlo Rosselli conceded fascism and its leader had emerged from the war greatly "reinforced and consolidated." Not only had Mussolini conceived the war and supervised every step in its preparation and execution, but he had displayed an impressive resolve in the face of opposition from his domestic allies and the western democracies. His gamble had paid off with a quick victory and a new Fascist empire at a tiny cost of Italian lives. As an added bonus, he had avenged the humiliation of Adowa and temporarily erased his people's sense of military inferiority. In the eyes of his adoring public, he had reestablished himself as a major figure in world affairs who had challenged the League of Nations, defied the British, and emerged victorious.

The Ethiopian War, however, also exposed Mussolini's limitations as a long-term planner and strategist on the global stage. The problems associated with his lack of long-term planning began to emerge after the occupation of Addis Ababa in the summer of 1936, when two-thirds of the new empire still remained outside Italian control. It soon became clear that the Duce had underestimated the difficulties of pacifying and controlling Ethiopia, a territory considerably larger than that of Italy. In the face of continued resistance outside Addis Ababa, Mussolini responded with extreme brutality. In July 1936 he ordered his chief representative in the colony, the newly created Fascist "Viceroy of Ethiopia," General Rodolfo Graziani, to initiate "a systematic policy of terror and extermination against rebels and any population who favors them." The secretary of the Fascist party, Starace, set the tone for the campaign by using groups of Ethiopian prisoners for target practice, first shooting them in the testicles before dispatching them with a shot to the heart. The Italian forces responded with renewed aerial bombardments, poison gas attacks, concentration camps, and mass executions of prisoners as well as Ethiopian intellectuals and teachers. This campaign of terror culminated in early 1937 after a failed attempt on Graziani's life in Addis Ababa. The Fascists retaliated with a murderous rampage that resulted in the deaths of several thousand Ethiopian civilians. Still the campaign of violence and reprisals did not achieve their primary objectives. By the end of 1937, the Italians still controlled only the railroad lines and the cities; elsewhere they continued to confront an active Ethiopian resistance.

More importantly, the Ethiopian War aroused international public indignation. Mussolini's unprovoked aggression against another country, his brutal methods of warfare, and his colonial atrocities permanently damaged his reputation and image in the world. The Duce, not Hitler, became the first European leader to resort to a war of aggression in the 1930s. He was also the first to unleash indiscriminate bombing and poison gas against a civilian population, in direct violation of the traditional norms of warfare. Above all, the Ethiopian War turned public opinion, especially in the western democracies, against Mussolini and fascism. Even many of his foreign sympathizers, who had once praised him as a heroic bulwark against communist revolution, now denounced him as an untrustworthy and irresponsible menace to peace and stability in Europe. Similarly, prominent western diplomats like the British foreign minister, Anthony Eden, asserted that "Mussolini has the mentality of a gangster." As Eden's comment suggests, the war marked a major break in the tradition of friendly relations between Italy and Great Britain.

Despite the Italian public's initial euphoria and excitement over victory in Ethiopia, the war's negative repercussions began to be felt at home as well. The war quickly proved to be a tremendous drain on Italy's limited economic and financial resources. From the outset, sanctions had caused the country to lose export markets in central and southern Europe. To make matters worse, the Duce had not paid much attention to the material costs of the war. They absorbed an entire year's national revenues, while the replacement of war materials employed in Ethiopia ate up the military budget for the next three years. Military and colonial expenses alone continued to account for more than half of all governmental expenditures throughout the second half of the decade. Not surprisingly, budgetary deficits mushroomed, increasing eightfold between 1934 and 1937, while prices for consumer goods soared. The sharp rise in public spending forced the regime, in turn, to scale back many of its domestic social programs and to introduce a series of new taxes that were unpopular with the middle classes and the wealthy.

The international hostility and economic difficulties at home created by the Ethiopian War did little to moderate the Duce's enthusiasm for an expansionist foreign policy. He displayed no interest in returning to a more conventional policy that permitted the consolidation of his new acquisitions and mending relations with Italy's traditional western allies. Mussolini's easy victory over a relatively defenseless foe and the ensuing adulation he received at home left him with an exalted sense of his country's real strength and of his own military prowess. Indeed, the outcome of the war convinced him that his true mission now lay in foreign affairs, where he saw himself predestined to lead Italy to "its appointment with history." The ineffectual responses of England and France to his aggression only reinforced his own ideological convictions that the western democracies were "age-weakened" powers in rapid decline and that he could pursue his dreams of a new Fascist empire in the Mediterranean and Red Sea at their expense. In his own mind, expansion abroad offered Mussolini benefits at home as well. Not only did it promise to loosen the restraints imposed by his conservative institutional allies, but it also offered a way to remold "the character of the Italians through combat," so that they would be "ready for the test" when a general European war inevitably arrived. Ominously, he dismissed the concerns of his advisers about the country's lack of military and economic preparation, confident that his own tactical brilliance would more than compensate for Italy's material shortcomings.

The Duce did not wait long before embarking on a new foreign adventure. Less than three months after the proclamation of the Ethiopian Empire, he plunged his country into the Spanish Civil War against the advice of the king and his military advisers. Much as in the case of Ethiopian War, Mussolini acted once again without any serious analysis of the political, economic, and diplomatic consequences of intervention. On July 30, 1936, he sent a squadron of Italian planes to bolster a two-week-old military revolt headed by General Francisco Franco against the democratic government of the Spanish Republic. When this initial aid did not lead to a quick victory by the military rebels, Mussolini steadily escalated Italy's military involvement during the fall. By the end of November, Mussolini had concluded a secret treaty with Franco, in which he agreed to dispatch Italian forces to the war front. In the following month, the first contingent of 7,800 Fascist volunteers and 2,200 regular troops had entered the fray. Their ranks swelled dramatically in the next few months so that by February 1937 the Duce had committed nearly 50,000 men to the war and made Italy the chief patron of the nationalist forces.

A combination of opportunism and ideology appears to have driven Mussolini's decision to intervene on the side of the right-wing Nationalists in the Spanish Civil War. On the one hand, he saw in the patronage of Franco an opportunity to exclude French influence in Spain, where they supported the Republican government, and increase dramatically his own power in the western Mediterranean at the expense of the British. This opportunity could be lost, he feared, if the Republic collapsed quickly or if Franco aligned with Nazi Germany rather than Fascist Italy. Accordingly, he acted immediately without consulting either the king or his advisers. On the other hand, the Duce also viewed Italian intervention in the civil war as part of a larger ideological struggle that pitted European fascism and its allies against the international forces of democracy, communist revolution, and antifascism. The arrival of Soviet Russian arms and advisers in the fall of 1936 only confirmed Mussolini's ideological reading of the conflagration. At least initially, the notion of a crusade against godless communism made it easier for him to sell intervention within Italy, especially among Italian Catholics.

The decision to intervene in the Spanish Civil War proved to be a decisive turning point for Mussolini and Italian Fascism. From the outset, the events in Spain exposed the Duce's profound limitations both as a diplomatic negotiator and as a military strategist. When his initial efforts on behalf of Franco did not result in an immediate victory over the Republican forces, Mussolini's preoccupation with his own prestige and image forced him to increase his financial and military involvement in the war, regardless of the consequences. By doing so, the Duce added to his growing reputation for diplomatic irresponsibility, since he had previously subscribed to an international nonintervention agreement in September 1936. To make matters worse, Franco outmaneuvered him at the negotiating table in November 1936. In exchange for unlimited Italian support on credit, Mussolini won little more than a vague promise of Spanish neutrality in the event of a war with a third power. In contrast, while Nazi Germany also provided air support for the Nationalists, Hitler limited his involvement in the civil war and exacted considerably more in economic concessions from Franco.

Mussolini's diplomatic shortcomings paled in comparison to the effects of his military dilettantism. Impatient with the slow pace of the war and eager to achieve a dramatic and decisive victory in the shortest time possible, he ordered his troops to advance as rapidly as possible toward the Spanish capital of Madrid. However, at the Battle of Guadalajara in March 1937, Spanish Republican units halted the advance of the Italian forces and then drove them into retreat. In this battle alone, Mussolini's troops suffered more casualties than during the entire Ethiopian War. Such a humiliating defeat delivered a permanent blow to the prestige of Mussolini and fascism. First of all, the rout exposed the glaring weaknesses of the Italian army and made a mockery of his claims about the new military superiority of the Fascist regime. Even worse from Mussolini's standpoint, it rekindled painful stereotypes about the inferior fighting abilities of the Italian people. Adding insult to injury, the humiliating defeat had been administered by antifascist volunteers, including many Italian political exiles, who celebrated the victory as a major setback to the cause of fascism.

Despite the defeat, Mussolini did not withdraw the Italian army from the war. He reportedly told one of his advisers after he got word of the battle: "There is no way that I shall withdraw any men from Spain until both the military and political failure of Guadalajara is avenged." With his own prestige and the reputation of his regime on the line, he intensified his country's engagement in what became a protracted and costly war of attrition in Spain. Much as he had done in Africa, the Duce displayed little concern for international law or humanitarian considerations in his methods of warfare. Once again, he called for the summary execution of prisoners of war and personally ordered the indiscriminate bombing of major cities like Barcelona to terrorize the civilian population into submission. Even with these methods, it still took another two years before the Nationalists entered Madrid and won control in the spring of 1939. By then, Mussolini had deployed more than 75,000 Italian troops and vast quantities of war supplies to Spain in support of the Nationalists.

Fascist propagandists proclaimed that Franco's triumph over the Republicans represented a great ideological victory for the Italian regime, since Spain was now ostensibly in the Fascist camp and the Soviet Union had been deprived of a foothold in the western Mediterranean. Unlike in Ethiopia, however, victory in Spain exacted an unanticipated price in casualties, weaponry, and revenue. Mussolini himself conceded that the war had "bled his country white." The three-year bloodbath resulted in nearly 16,000 Italian casualties and the loss of roughly a third of the country's available armaments; it wound up costing twice as much as Italy's total annual military budget. The prolonged military campaign also exacted a price on the homefront, where by the end of 1937 the war had become increasingly unpopular. Nor did the war improve Mussolini's standing abroad. If anything, public opinion in the west became even more convinced that he was an enemy of peace and democracy and a natural ally of the Nazis. Furthermore, the new regime in Spain did not offer Italy financial compensation or any preferential treatment in its economic and foreign policies. Thus, Fascist Italy received no tangible benefit from its costly engagement in the civil war.

Fascism's adventures abroad also exacted a high physical and psychological price on Mussolini himself. Already in 1936, some of his closest associates began to note signs of his physical decline. Despite a rigorous diet, his weight steadily rose, while his vision deteriorated. Others voiced concern about his state of mind, noting his growing isolation from the outside world. As one of the top figures in the regime, Italo Balbo, expressed it, the Duce "saw and felt nothing of reality." After an interview with Mussolini, another observer described him as "a sad figure, alone, despite all his glory." Surrounded by admirers and adoring subordinates, he began to believe in his own infallibility and became intolerant of any criticism or difference of opinion. In this context, setbacks and failures in foreign policy did not lead him to a more realistic assessment of his country's strategic interests and its limitations. On the contrary, they only seemed to magnify his commitment to ideological and military confrontation and to fuel even more wildly ambitious projects both at home and abroad. Since "the Duce is always right," the poverty of his accomplishments as a great statesman could not possibly be his own doing, but rather had to be the product of incompetent underlings or treacherous foreign enemies.

Mussolini had originally embarked on an aggressive new foreign policy in order to escape the constraints imposed on Italy by the post-Great War diplomatic system and to increase his power and prestige in the world. In doing so, he applied to the international arena the same combination of opportunism, ruthlessness, and tactical flexibility that had served him so well in Italian politics. After two wars, however, it became increasingly evident that Mussolini had not only tarnished his reputation in the world, he had exchanged one set of constraints for another. His open violation of international agreements, his recourse to naked aggression, and his brutal methods of warfare had alienated public opinion in the western democracies and created a widening breach with Italy's traditional allies, France and England. The Duce now found that he had even less freedom of action than before. As his relations with the western democracies steadily deteriorated after 1935, strategic necessity and ideological affinities led him to embrace a fateful alliance with Nazi Germany.

VIII

Mussolini and Hitler

1936–1940

Mussolini's alliance with Adolf Hitler defined his international reputation and public image in the twentieth century. The partnership between Fascist Italy and Nazi Germany in the late 1930s illustrates the enormous power the Duce exercised in foreign policy in the second decade of his rule, power that allowed him to impose his will on his country and its people. Against the wishes of his principal allies and the majority of ordinary Italians, he tied the fortunes of his regime and nation to Hitler and his plans for world conquest. At the same time, the consequences of this alliance illustrate the limitations of the Duce's charismatic style of leadership and his political methods when he applied them on the international stage. As a result, Mussolini bears overwhelming responsibility for the decisions that led his country down the path to a general war that would end in military catastrophe and foreign occupation, the collapse of the Fascist regime, and ultimately his own violent death at the hands of the antifascist resistance.

Fascism and Nazism displayed obvious affinities from their inception in the turbulent political environment of postwar Europe. To begin with, the two authoritarian movements combined a contradictory mix of an enthusiasm for modern technology with an idealization of traditional social relations. Both movements also adopted a new paramilitary style of mass politics that glorified the use of violence and employed distinctive uniforms, salutes, and banners to capture the public's attention. Through their violent campaign against the socialist labor movement in their respective countries, they attracted the support of the angry middle classes as well as frightened upper-class conservatives. On the ideological plane, both movements shared a hostility toward socialism, liberal democracy, and the postwar international order. Each embraced the rhetoric of extremist nationalism, militarism, and imperial expansion.

The kinship between fascism and Nazism also found expression in the personal bond that existed between their respective leaders. Although the balance of power in the relationship between Mussolini and Hitler shifted over time, the two dictators always maintained a powerful connection that profoundly influenced relations between the two countries. Throughout the 1920s, Mussolini, the triumphant ruler of Italy, remained the senior figure and role model for Hitler, who assumed the subordinate role of admirer and supplicant. While the majority of the Nazis tended to view Italians as racial inferiors, unreliable allies, and poor soldiers, Hitler steadfastly defended the Duce and Italian fascism in the years after the March on Rome. From the outset, he saw the Italian regime as a natural ally that shared his hostility to France and whose Mediterranean ambitions coincided with his own expansionist goals on the continent. Likewise, he recognized that the presence of the Fascist regime in Italy favored the rise of the Nazis. Even in the early 1940s he still insisted on the powerful influence of Italian developments on the Nazi movement, noting how "the brown shirt [Nazi] would not have existed without the black shirt" and asserting that the March on Rome "was one of the turning points in history." In the 1920s, Hitler was even more effusive in his admiration for the "incomparable" Mussolini, whom he praised as the "first statesman of the world." In homage to his mentor, Hitler displayed a bronze bust of the Duce in his party's headquarters in Munich.

For his part, Mussolini did not reciprocate the Nazi leader's admiration in the decade before Hitler's accession to power in 1933. He tended, instead, to view Hitler as a rather ridiculous figure, a crude and unrefined fanatic who lacked the personal qualities to become a great political leader. The Duce also displayed little enthusiasm for some of Hitler's ideas, once dismissing his political testament, *My Struggle*, as a "boring book which I have never been able to read." On the whole, Mussolini considered Hitler "a muddle-headed fellow; his brain is stuffed with philosophical and political tags that are utterly incoherent."

Above all, the Duce rejected the Nazi leader's pseudoscientific theories of Aryan superiority as "racial delirium." He certainly did not share Hitler's ferocious hatred of Jews. While Mussolini indulged in the sort of ethnic stereotyping common to his generation of Europeans, he showed few signs of a particular bias against Jews in either his private or his public life. His longtime mistress, Margherita Sarfatti, for instance, came from a Venetian Jewish family. Before 1933, he frequently condemned anti-Semitism on the grounds that Italian Jews had "always behaved well as citizens and fought courageously as soldiers." In fact, a number of Jews were founding members of the first *fascio di combattimento* in 1919, while others assumed prominent positions in the Fascist regime, serving in the cabinet, chamber of deputies, party, and state bureaucracy. Finally, as leader of a Catholic country, the Duce could hardly support Nazi proposals for euthanasia and sterilization of the mentally and physically handicapped.

Mussolini's personal reservations about Hitler, his Pan-German goals, and his racial theories did not prevent the Fascist regime from providing propagandistic support and strategic advice to the Nazis and other right-wing groups in the 1920s. The Italian dictator took even more interest after the stunning electoral advance of the Nazis in the early 1930s. In fact, the Fascists appeared pleased and hopeful about the large vote for Hitler's party, which they interpreted as a validation of their own ideological crusade against democratic liberalism and socialism. Thus, the Italian media portrayed Nazi victories as a major sign that "the fascist idea is moving ahead in the world." Meanwhile, secret contacts between Hitler and Mussolini's personal representative increased. When the Nazi leader came to power in January 1933, the Duce boasted confidently that "the victory of Hitler is also our victory." Two months later, he told one of his associates that he intended to forge "the closest contact between the Fascist and Nazi regimes" and authorized his representatives to undertake secret negotiations for cooperation with Germany.

Still the Fascist government remained uncomfortable with the fanaticism and dogmatism of the Nazis after Hitler came to power in January 1933. In fact, relations between the two dictatorships remained tense over the next two years largely as a result of Italian concerns about Nazi ambitions in Austria. As early as the mid-1920s, Mussolini had proclaimed his firm opposition to any border changes that would lead to Germany's annexation of Austria, a position that he reasserted in the ensuing years. Shortly after Hitler's accession to power, the Duce became the chief patron of the conservative, but anti-Nazi, chancellor of Austria, Engelbert Dollfuss, publicly promising his client that "in the defense of [Austria's] independence as a sovereign state, it can rely on us." Toward this end, he took the lead in creating a western coalition against German expansion that culminated in February 1934, when the British, French, and Italian governments issued statements in which they jointly reaffirmed the need for Austrian independence.

Hitler's stubborn refusal to compromise on the Austrian question sabotaged the first face-to-face meeting in Venice between the two dictators in June 1934 and set the stage for a major confrontation the next month. Although Hitler forswore any immediate annexation of his southern neighbor, he called for the Duce to withdraw his protection from Austria and demanded the removal of Dollfuss from the chancellor's office as a prelude to the introduction of Austrian Nazis into the government in Vienna. To make matters worse, the Nazi leader rambled on in German to his barely comprehending Italian host about the superiority of the Aryan race and the subversive activities of German Catholics. Mussolini commented after the meeting that Hitler had performed like "a gramophone with just seven tunes and once he had finished playing them he started all over again." Tensions over the Austrian question came to a head on July 25, 1934, when local Nazis assassinated Dollfuss in a failed coup attempt in Vienna. The Duce reacted to the murder of his protege as a personal affront, especially since it occurred on the eve of a scheduled meeting between the two men at a resort on Italy's Adriatic coast. In fact, Dollfuss' wife and children were already guests of the Mussolini family, who had to break the terrible news to them. A furious Duce denounced Hitler as a "horrible sexual degenerate" and immediately mobilized Italian troops and aircraft on the Austrian border.

While the Nazi leader publicly distanced himself from the assassination and halted all plans for direct intervention in Austria in its aftermath, the incident poisoned relations between the two dictatorships into 1935. During this period, Mussolini and the Fascist press openly criticized the German regime and ridiculed its ideas. The Duce proclaimed to one audience of Italians his "utter disdain [for] certain doctrines from the other side of the Alps by people who were illiterate at a time when Rome had Caesar, Virgil and Augustus." Similarly, he dismissed Nazi racial theories as "100% racism. Against all and everybody. Yesterday against Christian civilization; today against Latin civilization; tomorrow, who knows, against the civilization of the whole world." More importantly, the Dollfuss assassination sparked the formation of a three-power front whose principal purpose was to contain German expansion into Central Europe. To this end, the governments of England, France, and Italy issued a new joint statement in September 1934 reiterating their commitment to the independence of Austria. This agreement provided the basis for a broader anti-German alliance, the so-called Stresa Front, in the spring of 1935.

Developments in 1935 and 1936, however, brought about a fundamental change in relations between Fascist Italy and Nazi Germany. The reluctance of the western democracies to take a tough stand against Hitler alarmed the Duce, who complained after the Dollfuss assassination that he could not "always be the only one to march to the Brenner. Others must show some interest in Austria and the Danube basin." Moreover, their apparent willingness to make concessions to Nazi Germany reinforced his conviction that Britain and France were decadent, declining powers. Disappointment with the western democracies turned into anger and resentment when his European allies refused to approve Mussolini's imperial adventure in Africa. The Ethiopian War and the ensuing economic sanctions created an enormous breach between the Fascist regime and the west. As a result, the Duce became increasingly convinced of the need for a powerful, like-minded ally who could provide him with the military and economic support to break out of his "imprisonment" in the Mediterranean.

The Nazi regime skillfully exploited the divisions within the Stresa Front, playing on Italy's growing sense of isolation to bring Mussolini into a new and much closer relationship with Germany, based on the shared international interests and ideological affinities of the two dictatorships. From the outset, Hitler supported the Duce's war in Ethiopia precisely to widen the gulf between Italy and the west and to isolate the Fascist regime internationally. Accordingly, Germany refused to join the ranks of the countries that imposed economic sanctions on Italy in the

Mussolini and Hitler
meet in Rome in
1938 to solidify the
Rome-Berlin Axis

fall of 1935 and became one of the first countries to recognize officially Mussolini's new
African empire in June 1936. Support evolved
into more active collaboration later the same
summer, when the two dictatorships intervened
in the Spanish Civil War on the side of Franco
and the Nationalist insurgents. At the same time,
Hitler initiated a series of meetings between Nazi
and Fascist officials in the fall of 1936, in which
the Germans advocated closer ideological and
military cooperation against the twin threats of
"bolshevism" and western democracy.

In the altered international climate created by
the Ethiopian War, Mussolini took the lead in
pursuing a much closer collaboration with Nazi
Germany. As early as the fall of 1935, he renewed secret contacts with Hitler via trusted intermediaries that paved the way for a temporary
resolution of the divisive Austrian question. In
January 1936, the Duce encouraged Hitler to
transform Austria into "a satellite of Germany,"
an arrangement that preserved the facade of
Austrian independence and thereby allowed Italy
to save face. Later the same month he held out
the prospect of a much broader collaboration
between the two like-minded regimes. In a conversation with another emissary of Hitler's, he
asserted that Italy and Germany shared "a community of destiny" and predicted that "one day
we shall meet . . . . Because we must."

By the fall of 1936, the Duce gave the first
public indications of a major shift in Italo-German
relations. In September he began to promote the
idea of another face-to-face meeting with his
Nazi counterpart in order to "signal not just the
solidarity between the two regimes, but also a
common policy by the two states which must be
clearly delineated towards East and West, South
and North." While no such meeting took place
until the following year, Mussolini's foreign minister and son-in-law, Galeazzo Ciano, did go in

October to Germany, where he suggested to Hitler that the two regimes adopt a more aggressive approach toward the western democracies in order to shift the balance of power in Eastern Europe and the Mediterranean. These conversations set the stage for the Duce's announcement of a new understanding between Fascist Italy and Nazi Germany at the beginning of November. Addressing an audience of the Fascist faithful in front of the great cathedral in Milan, he proclaimed that the two states now constituted "an axis around which all European states . . . can revolve."

Even after his coining of the term Rome-Berlin Axis, the Duce maintained that he was still open to diplomatic overtures from the British, and he signed a "gentlemen's agreement" with London in January 1937, in which he promised to preserve the status quo in the Mediterranean. However, Mussolini's actions made a mockery of such diplomatic initiatives. His regime's continued involvement in the Spanish Civil War, a virulent anti-British campaign in the Fascist press, and his attempts to exploit Arab anti-imperial sentiments by promoting himself as the protector of Islam within Britain and France's Middle Eastern protectorates made it clear that he had no intention of restoring more cordial relations with the western democracies.

In fact, ideology, rather than pragmatic realism, guided Mussolini's foreign and domestic policies in the last years before World War II. The resulting radicalization of the Fascist regime coincided with the Duce's growing fascination with Hitler. By 1937, the old disdain for his German counterpart had been replaced by a new awe and fear of Hitler's enormous power and ruthlessness. Mussolini's first state visit to Germany in September of that year signaled a major shift in his relations with his fellow dictator. The carefully choreographed display of Germany's military might, industrial power, and mass regimentation dazzled the Duce. Above all, it confirmed his belief that the future success of his regime lay in a much closer affiliation with the Nazi regime.

Early in 1937 Mussolini began to move toward an alliance with Germany by displaying greater flexibility on the Austrian question. In April, he talked about the need for "synchronizing and harmonizing" the situation in Austria "with the Rome-Berlin Axis." More concretely, Mussolini announced in November 1937 that his regime had joined Germany and Japan in the Anti-Comintern Pact, an alliance directed against the Soviet Union and the international communist movement. In the following month he took his country out of the League of Nations, charging that the international body was in the hands of "occult forces opposed to our Italy and our revolution."

Mussolini's growing admiration for Hitler and his regime also produced a new determination to instill in the Italian people the qualities of strength and discipline that had impressed him about the Germans during his visit. Accordingly, he launched a campaign at home to transform "the character of Italians" by means of more militaristic policies modeled on those of Nazi Germany. An obvious example of such emulation was the introduction of the Nazi "goose-step," a high and stiff-legged marching stride, for all parades in February 1938. Mussolini justified the move on the grounds that it "expresses an authentic militarism." To those who charged that he was simply imitating the Germans, the Duce replied that what he called the *"passo romano,"* or Roman step, had its origins in the ancient legions of Italy's own Roman Empire. In another move to make his people "ready for conflict," he ordered all state employees in 1938 to follow the lead of the armed forces and wear uniforms adorned with badges indicating their rank in the bureaucracy. The Fascist party even went so far as to launch a heavily publicized drive to purify the Italian language by eliminating all foreign words and phrases from public discourse.

Neither Mussolini's new friendship with Hitler nor his measures to militarize his regime at home met with much favor from his conservative allies, Fascist officials, or the Italian public in general. For his part, Victor Emanuel III made no secret of his dislike for Germans and for the Nazis in particular. According to one source, the king harbored a special dislike for Hitler, whom he viewed as a "degenerate," addicted to narcotics and stimulants. Pope Pius XI was even more outspoken in his opposition to the Axis. In January 1937, the pope issued a ringing condemnation of Nazi ideology, morality, and programs. During a state visit by Hitler to Rome the following year, Pius registered his disapproval by closing the Vatican's museums and withdrawing to his villa in the countryside. Economic concerns led Italian industrial interests to oppose Mussolini's growing friendship with the Nazi regime. They feared the loss of state protection from their powerful German competitors within Italy and in Central Europe. Even within the leadership of the Fascist party itself, the pro-German elements constituted a small minority, while the rest either had reservations or were hostile to the direction of the regime's foreign policy. Finally, the larger Italian public remained fearful that an alliance with the Nazi regime would increase the risk of a general war.

The unilateral actions of Hitler and his regime in the spring of 1938 did not make the idea of the Rome-Berlin Axis any more attractive to the Italian people. Although he already had tacitly agreed to Germany's taking Austria, the Duce received only one day's notice before the Nazis invaded and annexed that country in mid-March. Mussolini justified the annexation by claiming that the new friendship between his regime and Nazi Germany meant that Italy no longer needed an independent Austria on her northern border. Nonetheless, Hitler's invasion damaged Mussolini's image at home. As the reports of his prefects testified, all segments of Italian society, rich and poor, Fascist and non-fascist, viewed the Nazi annexation as a major setback for the dictatorship. To make matters worse, the Duce's meek acceptance of it damaged his personal popularity and prestige, since it left the impression both with the Italian people and in the larger international community that he had become a junior partner in his relationship with Hitler.

Domestic discontent with the Rome-Berlin Axis did little to restrain Mussolini or lead him to reconsider his relationship with Nazi Germany. On the contrary, internal criticism and dissent only seemed to infuriate him and stiffen his resolve to push forward with his pro-German policies. On the home front, the Duce directed much of his anger toward his reluctant partners in the regime: the monarchy, the church, and the propertied elites. The monarchy, he informed his closest collaborators, had become an unnecessary burden on the regime and needed to be eliminated. While Mussolini did not actively pursue this goal, he did attempt to undermine the authority of the monarchy by having himself elevated in March 1938 to the rank of First Marshal of the Empire. As a consequence, he became the official commander of the Italian armed forces in wartime, a role previously reserved for the king. In a similar vein, Mussolini threatened to launch a new anti-clerical campaign against the Vatican and to unleash a "third wave" of Fascist revolution against the "defeatist" propertied classes, who needed, in his view, "three good kicks in the stomach." Nor was the Duce's anger and frustration limited to his conservative allies. Indeed, he insisted that the Italian people in general still displayed "an excessive individualism, an exaggerated sentimentalism, [and] a lack of calm and tenacity." They had to become "hard, relentless, and hateful—in fact, masters."

Mussolini moved closer to an alliance with the Nazis in the summer of 1938 when he began to promote his new doctrines on race and anti-Semitism to the Italian public. Without any prompting from the Nazis, the campaign officially kicked off in July with the publication of the *Manifesto of Racial Scientists*, a document consisting of ten statements, to which he contributed personally. In a sharp departure from his previous views, the Duce now insisted that "the people of Italy are of Aryan origin and their civilization is Aryan." More ominously, the document went on to affirm that "the Jews do not belong to the Italian race." The *Manifesto of Racial Scientists* laid the ideological foundations for a series of racial laws that Mussolini introduced in the following months. In August the government banned foreign-born Jews from Italian schools. Three months later additional laws forbade the "marriage of an Italian citizen of Aryan race to a person belonging to another race" and excluded Jews from employment in the army, schools, banking and insurance, and the state and party bureaucracies. The same legislation also prohibited them from owning more than 50 hectares of land or companies with more than 100 employees. Additional decrees in 1939 prevented them from working as journalists and public notaries. As a consequence, Italy's Jewish community, which numbered little more than 48,000 people, was excluded from virtually all forms of productive economic activity, forced to sell their property, or else compelled to make private arrangements with "Aryan" friends.

A combination of personal resentments and political opportunism led to Mussolini's decision to incorporate racism and anti-Semitism into the program and policies of Italian fascism. The Duce's interest in issues of race and the status of Jews first emerged during his military campaign in Africa. As early as 1936, he began to comment angrily about the large number of Jews in the antifascist movement and in the foreign press corps that was so harshly critical of his invasion of Ethiopia. At the same time, the need to define social relations between Italians and Africans within the newly acquired empire raised the profile of racial issues in general. The birth of a growing number of mixed-race children, in particular, alarmed Mussolini and led him to demand the imposition of "racial discipline" in the colonies. By 1937, he had laws enacted in Ethiopia to protect the supposed racial superiority of the Italian conquerors. They compelled Italians and Africans to live in separate areas and travel on different means of public transport. Additional legislation imposed harsh penalties on Italians who lived with a black "subject" and precluded any recognition of mixed-race children.

While anger over the perceived antifascism of the Jewish community and social concerns in the colonies helped lay the ideological groundwork for the racial laws, short-term diplomatic and domestic political considerations largely determined their character and the timing of Mussolini's decision to introduce them in 1938. On the one hand, the Duce saw state-sponsored anti-Semitism as a way to strengthen his relationship with Germany by eliminating one of the last major differences between Fascism and Nazism. The racial laws sent a clear signal to Hitler and to the western democracies of his own ruthlessness and of his firm commitment to the Rome-Berlin Axis. On the other hand, Mussolini also viewed the racial laws as a powerful instrument on the home front to force his reluctant institutional allies into line and to bring his people closer to the ideal of the tough "new fascist man."

The propagandistic character of Mussolini's racial legislation found expression in the ways that it was implemented. From the outset, Fascist anti-Semitism displayed little of the biological determinism and fanatic hatred of Nazi racial policies. Despite all their talk of Italian racial purity, the Fascists employed a looser definition of Jewish identity than their Nazi colleagues, limiting it to three groups: those individuals whose parents were both Jewish, those who had a Jewish father and a foreign-born mother, and those from mixed marriages who professed the Jewish religion. In addition, Mussolini's legislation exempted a wide array of people from persecution.

Among those who received exemptions were Jewish converts of mixed marriages, older foreign Jews, foreign Jews who had married Italians, Jewish veterans of the Great War or other wars, and Jewish "Fascists of the first hour." Finally, the Duce had a special law passed that gave him the authority to "Aryanize" whomever he pleased.

Nonetheless, the Fascist regime's racial legislation encountered a hostile reception abroad and aroused little enthusiasm at home. Only Nazi Germany, a few allied states in southeastern Europe, and some Arab countries reacted favorably to the legislation. Within Italy, the massive propaganda campaign in favor of the racial laws failed to win over any significant segment of the population. While the monarchy and the Catholic church had their own anti-Semitic tendencies, neither institution greeted the new measures excluding Jews from public life with much favor. Victor Emanuel III signed the exclusionary legislation into law, but privately he voiced concerns about a program that seemed to ape that of Germany. As the king told the Duce's son-in-law, he could not understand "how a great man like [Mussolini] can import these racial fashions from Berlin into Italy . . . . He must understand that if he falls into the German rut, he will range against himself the Church, the bourgeoisie, and the army high command." In fact, the Catholic hierarchy objected to the marriage sections of the legislation and the treatment of the Jewish community as a race rather than a religion. Nor did the best efforts of the Fascist propagandists succeed in whipping up much mass enthusiasm for racial ideas and laws that ran counter to popular traditions of tolerance. Countless Italians quietly refused to support or participate in their implementation either on humanitarian grounds or else because they saw them as another step in the direction of an alliance with Germany and war.

The modest results of the Fascist campaign on behalf of the racial legislation reflected a larger failure of the regime to arouse much mass support for the Rome-Berlin Axis and European war. In particular, the constant rallies, marches, and ceremonies promoted by the Fascist party in 1938 and 1939 proved counterproductive. Instead of engendering enthusiasm in the population, they tended to produce mounting exhaustion, annoyance, and resentment. The resulting climate of disrespect, sarcasm, and ridicule did not threaten the survival of fascism, but it served to discredit the party and the regime in the eyes of a growing number of Italians.

The Duce's failure to win over the hearts and minds of his people to his new foreign and domestic policies did not lead him to try to restrain the expansionist ambitions of his Axis partner.

The dust had hardly settled after the Nazi annexation of Austria when Hitler provoked a new crisis. Late in the spring of 1938, he demanded that his eastern neighbor, Czechoslovakia, hand over to Germany one of its strategically vital border regions, the Sudetenland, on the grounds that it had a large German population. Nazi officials once again treated their Fascist colleagues as subordinates, refusing repeated requests to share German military plans. For his own part, Mussolini initially appeared ready to risk war over the Sudetenland, but then gave up the idea in the absence of Italian military preparation, the support of public opinion, and the backing of the monarchy and army. Nonetheless, he desperately wanted to preserve his tattered image as a warrior and to convince Hitler of his commitment to the Rome-Berlin Axis. His solution to this dilemma was to indulge in a warlike rhetoric without taking any measures to prepare his country for the eventuality of war. Thus he boldly assured his foreign minister in May that, if the Czech crisis led to hostilities, he would immediately go to war on the side of Nazi Germany, a position that he reasserted throughout the summer of 1938. Yet his government remained the only major power in Europe to take virtually no military precautions or make preparations even as the crisis came to a head in September.

The Duce's willingness to stand shoulder to shoulder with Hitler and risk a war his country was not ready to fight rested upon his ideologically driven assumptions about the western "demoplutocracies." They represented the "old" civilization of Europe that was doomed to decay and decline. Demographic weakness, in his view, had sapped the English and French of their former dynamism and made them fearful of sacrifices and incapable of engaging in a war, especially against what Mussolini hailed as "the most formidable military-political combine that has ever existed." Accordingly, he gambled that they would capitulate to Hitler's territorial demands for the Sudetenland and he would not have to honor his promise to support Germany militarily. As he confidently put it, "swallowing pills is what democracies are made for." At the end of September 1938, Mussolini's gamble paid off when the British and French backed down and invited him to mediate the dispute with Germany. The Duce persuaded Hitler to convene a conference of the four great powers in the German city of Munich on September 29. There the western democracies abandoned their Czech ally by agreeing to the Nazi occupation of the Sudetenland.

In the short run, the Munich Conference represented a major personal triumph for Mussolini, who emerged from it with his popularity and prestige as an international statesman greatly enhanced. A grateful Britain and France rewarded him for his role as diplomatic arbiter by finally recognizing Italy's Ethiopian empire. Closer to home, enthusiastic crowds greeted him as a national hero and the "savior of the peace" upon his return from Munich. Such spontaneous displays of popular adulation irritated Mussolini, however, since they rested upon his role as peacemaker and revealed a widespread joy and relief that war had been avoided. In this respect, they provided new evidence that his program to militarize Italian society and harden his people into fearless warriors had made very little progress.

More importantly, his successful gamble at Munich reinforced dangerous illusions in Mussolini about his ability to override domestic opposition, support Hitler's expansionist ambitions in Eastern Europe, and achieve his own territorial ambitions in the Mediterranean while avoiding a general European war he was not ready to fight. In line with this approach, he used the Fascist press to pressure the French government into handing over to Italy the territories of "Tunis, Corsica, Nice, [and] Savoy" in November 1938. The same month he informed the Fascist Grand Council of his intentions to conquer Albania, push north into Switzerland, and expand into East Africa. Early the following year, he expanded his grandiose territorial ambitions to include Cyprus, Malta, Suez, and Gibraltar as part of a larger aim of breaking out into the Indian and Atlantic Oceans.

In sharp contrast to Hitler's precise war plans, Mussolini's expansionist projects lacked any clear time frame; he preferred instead to postpone their realization to a distant and undefined future. He did so with good reason, since the condition of the Italian armed forces and the Italian economy at the beginning of 1939 precluded any major military operations in the short term. While the Duce had boasted of more than 150 divisions and 12 million soldiers at his disposal, he was in fact bluffing. In 1939, his military preparations lagged well behind those of the other great powers. He had only ten divisions and some 160,000 soldiers ready to fight and virtually no reserves, while much of the army's equipment was nonexistent, inadequate, or obsolete. The armored divisions, for instance, possessed 20-year-old armored cars and had no tanks. Likewise, the air force was "irremediably out of date" and the navy little more than a "cardboard fleet." At the same time, the costs of two wars and an expanded colonial empire had taken a heavy toll on the Italian economy by the late 1930s. Mussolini's finance officials warned him that his nation's economy was precarious and could not support any new burdens, let alone a major war. Falling revenues from tourism and severe shortages of essential raw materials finally forced the Fascist government in 1939 to sell a portion of its already inadequate arms production to its ideological adversaries.

Mussolini's military posturing failed to win any territorial concessions from Britain and France in the Mediterranean or to impress his German partner in the last year before World War II. Discussions with the British government in the winter of 1938–1939 did little to weaken the Anglo-French alliance or resolve any outstanding differences between Italy and the western democracies. To make matters much worse, the Duce discovered once again that he exercised little influence over Hitler. On March 15, 1939, the Nazis invaded and occupied the rest of Czechoslovakia without prior consultation with their Axis partner. Mussolini learned of the invasion only when he received a message from the German leader after the fact. He initially reacted to the news with anger and alarm, but these emotions soon gave way to a mix of pessimism and fatalism.

The Duce's preoccupation with his personal grudges and with his image as the all-knowing leader prevented him from changing course and thus limited his diplomatic options in the spring of 1939. While Hitler had treated him as a vassal rather than an equal partner, Mussolini had already committed his country to the Axis, and a break with Nazi Germany would have meant an unacceptable loss of face at home. Such a change of course would have entailed a tacit admission that the Duce had been wrong all along and that the voices of caution in the Fascist hierarchy, the Catholic church, the monarchy, and the business world were justified in their opposition to the Rome-Berlin Axis. In any case, Mussolini had no intention of abandoning his own imperial ambitions in order to mend fences with his hated enemies in the west. Moreover, he remained convinced that Germany's demographic strength and military might made her an irresistible force that was destined, with or without Italy, to dominate Europe.

Trapped in an ideological and diplomatic prison largely of his own making, Mussolini plowed ahead with even more belligerent rhetoric and policies in the spring of 1939. Less than a month after the Nazi occupation of Czechoslovakia, the Duce ordered his armed forces to invade Albania. He did so in an attempt to assert his independence from Hitler and to impress the western democracies with a show of Italian force. His commanders received only one week's notice, so military operations began on April 7 with virtually no advance preparation. While the Albanians offered little armed resistance to the invaders, shortages of equipment and problems of organization led to chaos and confusion, providing further evidence to friends and foes of Italy's military weakness. The conquest of Albania did not improve Mussolini's bargaining position with Britain and France, who had become convinced that he had to be considered an enemy. The British government responded by introducing the military draft, guaranteeing military support to Greece and Turkey against Italy, and strengthening its own positions in Egypt and Malta. Furthermore, the new conquest aroused no patriotic fervor on the home front. The great majority of Italians greeted news of the invasion with alarm.

Nevertheless, Mussolini upped the diplomatic stakes the following month when he committed his country to an offensive pact with Nazi Germany without first consulting his own ministers or military experts. The previous fall, the Duce had informed German representatives that he saw no need for a defensive agreement between the two dictatorships, since "no one thinks of attacking the totalitarian states." He envisioned instead an alliance "to change the map of the world." In line with this vision, Mussolini signed a treaty with Germany, the Pact of Steel, on May 7, 1939. According to its terms, he agreed to a full military alliance with Nazi Germany that required Italy to support its ally with "all its military forces on land, on sea, and in the air" even in the event that Hitler unleashed an unprovoked attack on another country.

From Mussolini's embattled perspective, the Pact of Steel offered emotional and practical rewards. It sent a loud and clear message to his "defeatist" colleagues in Italy that he was in charge and that there would be no turning back from the path he had taken. Within Europe, it provided a vehicle for expressing his anger toward the western democracies who had frustrated his dreams of dominance in the Mediterranean. And the military alliance served to reassure Nazi Germany that he remained a loyal ally worthy of their respect and support. While Mussolini insisted that a European conflict was "inevitable," he convinced himself that, in exchange for his commitment to an alliance, the Nazis would postpone any war plans until the end of 1942. An extended period of peace, he informed his German ally, was essential so that the Fascist government could prepare domestic public opinion, consolidate its recent colonial conquests in Africa and the Balkans, reequip its army, and expand its naval fleet.

The Nazis soon dispelled Mussolini's illusions that the Pact of Steel had won him an equal partnership with Hitler or an extended period of peace. In mid-June 1939, German propagandists began to intensify their verbal attacks on Poland. Meanwhile, Hitler secretly ordered his military to prepare for an invasion of his eastern neighbor that he planned to launch in a matter of months. Mussolini, for his part, remained oblivious to warnings from his own diplomats and did little either to halt the drift toward war or to accelerate the pace of Italian military preparations. The reality of the situation did not hit home until mid-August, when Germany had rejected the Duce's proposals for a new peace conference and made clear that the invasion of Poland would begin no later than the end of the month. Moreover, Hitler kept his Italian ally in the dark about negotiations with their mutual ideological enemy, Communist Russia, that concluded with the announcement of a Nazi-Soviet nonaggression pact on August 21, 1939.

The prospect of a European war erupting in a matter of days confronted Mussolini with an extremely painful dilemma. On the one hand, his own political prestige required that he honor his commitment to the Pact of Steel, which marked the culmination of nearly four years of Fascist warmongering and ideological posturing at home and abroad. On a less exalted plane, he feared that any abandonment of Nazi Germany at such a critical juncture would deprive Italy of a share in the potential rewards of a German victory. On the other hand, he was aware that Italy was not ready for an immediate war in 1939 that would only expose her military weakness and risk an even greater national humiliation. Apart from the woeful state of his Italian armed forces, he also knew he lacked the support of the Italian public and his key institutional allies for a policy of military intervention on the side of Nazi Germany.

At the end of August, the Duce adopted a compromise solution to the dilemma created by the Polish crisis. He promised to maintain his commitment to the Pact of Steel but keep his country out of the war for the time being. Mussolini attempted to conceal his backsliding by advancing impossible demands on his ally. He informed Hitler that he could participate in the conflict only if Germany furnished him with massive quantities of "war supplies and primary products" that would have required 17,000 trains filled with 170 million tons of goods. When the Germans predictably turned down these demands, he replied that he was "compelled by forces outside my control to withhold from you my active support in the hour of action."

Mussolini's decision was a popular one at home, where, according to his son-in-law, the people were "in absolute totality happy about the decisions which have been taken." The country's stock market soared in response to the news, the Vatican voiced its pleasure, and virtually all of the leading Fascists reacted with relief and satisfaction. Outside Italy, Mussolini's decision met with approval from his fellow dictators in Spain and Portugal, Franco and Antonio de Oliveira Salazar; even Hitler seemed content with his Fascist ally's "psychological backing." Indeed, in September 1939 the only person in Italy who seemed unhappy with the outcome of the crisis was Mussolini himself. Writing in his diary on the night of September 2, his son-in-law noted: "The Duce is convinced of the need to remain neutral, but he is not pleased by it. Every time he can, he refers to the possibility of action on our part."

IX

Death of a Regime and a Man

1940–1945

There is little doubt that Benito Mussolini was the principal architect of his country's shift from neutrality to armed intervention in World War II. In December 1940, British Prime Minister Winston Churchill asserted that "one man alone has ranged the Italian people in deadly struggle against the British Empire." In doing so that man had acted "against the Crown and Royal Family of Italy, against the Pope and all the authority of the Vatican and of the Roman Catholic Church, against the wishes of the Italian people who had no lust for this war."

From the outset, the Duce did not share in the general sense of relief felt by most Fascist leaders, his conservative institutional allies, and the wider Italian public at the prospect of avoiding the conflict. In September 1939, one of his close associates noted how he "speaks of 'neutrality' with horror [and as] a 'betrayal.'" Indeed, he appeared personally ashamed of Fascist Italy's place on the sidelines that seemed to belie the virile image he had of himself and his regime. As he lamented to his son-in-law, Count Ciano, in October, the Italian people "after hearing my warlike propaganda for eighteen years, cannot understand how I can become the herald of peace, now that Europe is in flames." Much as in the fall of 1914, Mussolini viewed neutrality as a cowardly posture that excluded his country from "great events" and betrayed its historical mission to act as a great power. In fact, he insisted on defining his regime's position in the fall of 1939 as one of "non-belligerence" to distinguish it from his Liberal predecessors' policy of "neutrality" at the beginning of the Great War. Of more practical significance, he refused to disavow the Pact of Steel or distance himself from the Nazis, against the advice of prominent Fascists as well as his military advisers and the court.

Despite his loyalty to the Rome-Berlin Axis and his emotional difficulties with nonbelligerence, the Duce could do little about the harsh economic and military realities that forced him to stay out of the war in September. The hope that a period of peace would give the regime time to overcome shortages in currency reserves, raw materials, and armaments did not materialize. The Italian economy continued to deteriorate in the winter of 1939–1940 as a consequence of the international situation and increased military expenditures. Government officials reported serious shortages of vital raw materials and basic necessities, while the state deficit continued to grow at an alarming rate. The rationing of especially scarce items like coffee and sugar and the requisitioning of iron did little to slow the rise in prices or the resulting deterioration of the standard of living for most Italians. Nor did the Duce's threats have much of a positive impact on the regime's military preparedness. The perennial inefficiency of the military bureaucracies, combined with shortages of strategic resources, machine tools, and skilled labor, sabotaged efforts to raise Italy's level of combat readiness in either Europe or Africa. In December 1939, the Duce received the discouraging news that neither the army nor the navy would be ready for war until at least 1943–1944.

These problems darkened Mussolini's mood and took their toll on his health in the winter of 1939–1940. His inability to enter the conflict on the side of Germany provoked mounting irritation that he increasingly directed against his own people. "The Italian race," he informed Ciano in February, "is a race of sheep. Eighteen years are not enough to change them. It takes a hundred and eighty, and maybe a hundred and eighty centuries." During the same period, Mussolini complained again of stomach pains, fueling rumors of his physical and emotional decline. After a visit with the Duce late in February, the American diplomat Sumner Welles recalled a deeply depressed Fascist leader: "The man I saw before me seemed fifteen years older than his actual age of fifty-six. He was ponderous and static rather than vital. He moved with an elephantine motion; every step appeared an effort. He was heavy for his height, and his face in repose fell in rolls of flesh. His close-cropped hair was snow white."

When Welles returned to Rome a few weeks later, however, he encountered a reinvigorated and more self-assured Mussolini. By then, the Duce had become convinced that his country must intervene in the European conflict on the side of Germany. At the beginning of March, Mussolini informed one of his top ministers, Giuseppe Bottai, that Italy would enter "either a war with Germany or a parallel war in pursuit of our own interests," a position that he reaffirmed in a letter to Hitler in mid-March. At that time he assured his Nazi allies that his country would join them "at the opportune moment" and spelled out his ambitious war aims in the Mediterranean at the expense of France and England.

Two circumstances accelerated Mussolini's move toward intervention in World War II. First, a tightening British blockade reduced imports of German coal and threatened to paralyze rearmament and suffocate Italian industry. Second, the prospect of an impending German military offensive in Western Europe convinced Mussolini that Fascist Italy must join the fray if it wanted to get a share of the spoils of war. He indicated as much in a late-night telephone conversation in mid-March with his mistress, Clara Petacci, in which he insisted that Italy must get into the conflict, since "Germany will win the war in the shortest possible time due to its great power and the quality of its troops and because of its amazing new weapons that are in an advanced stage of preparation." Count Ciano noted in his diary the same week how "the thought of war" dominated his father-in-law and would "dominate him even more, if the offensive on the western front begins." In Ciano's opinion, the Germans needed "no great power of oratory to urge on the Duce a course of action that he, the Duce, desires with all his soul."

Mussolini's commitment to intervention on the side of the Axis became increasingly evident in the spring of 1940. At the end of March, he told the king that a "parallel war" alongside Germany was inevitable. Early the next month,

he warned his governmental ministers that war
might begin at any moment, a war in which Italy
would acquire a "Mediterranean empire" and
"access to the [Atlantic] ocean." When the Nazis
invaded Norway and Denmark on April 9, Mussolini informed the German ambassador that he
endorsed "Hitler's action wholeheartedly" and
gave orders "to the press and to the Italian people to applaud unreservedly this German action." Nazi victories in Scandinavia not only
evoked his approval, but also whetted his own
appetite for military action. As he complained to
his son-in-law, "it is humiliating to remain with
our hands folded while others write history."
Fascist Italy, he argued, should "take advantage
of this occasion to pit our Navy against the
French and British forces." At the same time,
Mussolini and his propagandists displayed a noticeably cold stance toward overtures from the
western democracies. When the French prime
minister sent him a personal appeal for peace in
April, the Duce responded that his country
meant "to stay the political and military ally of
Germany in adherence to the Treaty of May
1939, a treaty which Italy, like all nations who
cherish their honor, intends to respect." He was
equally dismissive of peace initiatives advanced
by the American president, Roosevelt, at the beginning of May.

While important segments of the Fascist regime did not share his enthusiasm for war on the side of Nazi Germany, Mussolini's dominant position and his intolerance of criticism made it difficult for any of them to openly oppose his foreign policy or push an effective alternative in the spring of 1940. The cult of the Duce and the systematic subordination of the party to the dictator over the previous decade had inseparably linked Mussolini and fascism in the minds of most Italians. Ingrained habits of unconditional loyalty discouraged action by Fascist dissidents, who in any case feared that any opposition would appear as a betrayal of their infallible leader. Likewise, after nearly two decades of collaboration with Mussolini, the monarchy and the Catholic church were reluctant to risk the stability of the entire regime and their own established positions within it by provoking a direct confrontation with him over the war.

While Mussolini's ideological commitments, his need for action, and his territorial ambitions drove him toward intervention, more cynical, opportunistic calculations dictated his actual decision to enter the war in the summer of 1940. On May 10, Hitler launched his long-anticipated offensive in the west with the invasion of Holland and Belgium. The rapid advance of Nazi forces across France in the following weeks and the prospect of a quick victory for Germany in the west suddenly put the Duce in the position of having to intervene with an unprepared army. Otherwise he feared he would lose out on the martial glory, the spoils of victory, and an influential role in Hitler's new Europe. Mussolini understood, as he told one of his generals in late May, that if he "were to have the army ready, I would have to wait years before entering the war, while I must enter immediately." Germany's stunning successes on the battlefield seemed to reduce greatly the risks of Italian intervention. Mussolini was confident that any military campaign involving his forces would not last beyond September. Under these circumstances, he concluded that the Italian army's preparations were sufficient, especially since Fascist Italy needed, in his words, only "a few thousand dead to be able to attend the peace conference as a belligerent." As one general put it, the Duce aimed to "declare war, in order to not fight it, and then sit at the peace table as a belligerent in order to claim his share of the booty."

Hitler's rapid advance in the west also weakened domestic opposition to Italy's involvement in the conflict. By the end of May, the apparent inevitability of a German victory provoked a shift in public opinion away from overwhelming support for nonbelligerence to acceptance of, if not enthusiasm for, a war that promised to be very brief, require few sacrifices, and provide easy gains, as long as Italy did not "arrive late." Most prominent Fascists now abandoned their previous reservations about the war and the German alliance, along with industrialists who looked to gain a share of the potential spoils. Victor Emanuel III continued to have his doubts, warning that "those who talk of a short and easy war are deluding themselves," but he had become "resigned to the idea of war" and approved a declaration of hostilities. By June even the Catholic church accepted the idea of Italian involvement in a brief, victorious war.

Nonetheless, Mussolini made the final decision to enter the war. Without consulting either his cabinet or the Fascist Grand Council, he notified Hitler in early June that Italy would declare war on France and England one week later and begin hostilities the following day. To insure that he alone received all the glory of certain victory, the Duce took over as commander-in-chief of the Italian armed forces. On the evening of June 10, 1940, Mussolini made the official announcement to his people and the rest of the world from the balcony of his government office in Rome. Speaking to an audience of cheering party members mobilized for the occasion, he proclaimed that Fascist Italy was "going to war against the plutocratic and reactionary democracies of the west, who have always hindered the advance and often threatened the very existence of the Italian people." The goal of his war was clear: "We want to break the territorial and military chains that bind us in our own sea: a nation of forty-five million souls is not truly free unless it has free access to the ocean." At the same time, he cast his initiative in ideological terms as "the logical development of our revolution . . . the struggle of fertile, young peoples against sterile ones on the threshold of decline." He concluded his speech by exhorting all Italians to "rush to arms and show your tenacity, your courage, your valor!"

From the first day of Italy's involvement in the war, nothing seemed to work out according to Mussolini's expectations. Warning signs of impending disaster appeared almost immediately. Two hours before the formal declaration, the British navy attacked an Italian submarine. The following day Allied airplanes began a bombing campaign on Italy's northern industrial cities that exposed the weakness of Mussolini's anti-aircraft defenses. Despite the declaration of war, his troops did not launch an offensive against the French across the Alpine border between the two countries until after the Germans had entered Paris and France had requested an armistice. In this way, Mussolini managed to create the impression abroad of having cowardly attacked an already vanquished foe. Even then the four-day Alpine campaign encountered strong resistance from the French and succeeded in capturing only a couple of border towns, forcing a humiliated Mussolini to go to Munich with little leverage in the discussions of the peace settlement. Under the circumstances, Hitler was more interested in an advantageous settlement with the French and paid scant attention to his Italian colleague's demands. Not only did he reject the Duce's sweeping claims to French territories on the continent and in the Mediterranean, but he excluded him from joint peace negotiations with France. Italy did sign a separate armistice with France in late June, but he gained only the few acres of French territory taken during the brief campaign. Hitler also excluded his Italian allies from any role in the preparation of his impending invasion of the British Isles and ordered them to stay out of the Balkans. More seriously, Mussolini's short, easy war did not materialize as expected when the confrontation between the English and German air forces in the Battle of Britain failed to produce a decisive Nazi victory and an end to hostilities in the fall of 1940. Likewise, the Duce's pretensions to dominance in the Mediterranean suffered a major setback in November when the British fleet launched a surprise assault upon the Italian naval base at Taranto. The attack cost the Italians a number of ships, including three battleships.

The lack of results on the battlefield and at sea reflected in turn more fundamental problems of organization and leadership within the Fascist regime. In the first weeks of the war, one of the Duce's top lieutenants lamented the "failure of preparation" and the constant "improvisation" that characterized the entire undertaking. Since Mussolini had assumed that armed intervention would be brief, he did not bother to orchestrate a full-scale mobilization of the country's economy for war. Months after Italy's intervention in the conflict, large numbers of Italians remained out of work even in the major industrial centers of the north that produced armaments. By the end of 1940, the country's industry was still operating at a quarter of its modest capacity. Nor did the situation improve over time. Remarkably, the government did not create a ministry of war production until February 1943. In the absence of any mechanism to establish and impose military and economic priorities, the production of weapons and strategic materials like steel remained woefully inadequate, both in quantity and quality. Fascist Italy was the only combatant nation not to increase its gross domestic production between 1940 and 1942. The old military leadership compounded these problems with its outdated notions of warfare, its antiquated command structure, and its internal rivalries. In his role as commander-in-chief, Mussolini's erratic style of leadership did not help matters. His preoccupation with image over substance, his preference for dramatic gestures over long-range planning, and his ignorance of the logistical complexities of combat made him particularly ill-suited to deal with the enormous challenges of total war.

Mussolini managed to make the worst of a bad situation by spreading his already inadequate military forces over a number of fronts in the stubborn pursuit of his "parallel war" in the Mediterranean and North Africa during the fall of 1940. Without consulting his German allies, he launched an unprovoked attack on Greece on October 28 to compensate for his lack of territorial gains and loss of prestige in the summer. His own military leaders received only two weeks notice about the operation and thus had little time to plan or prepare for it. The Duce, for his part, displayed scant concern for war preparations. In his view, the inferior Greeks could not mount serious resistance to the forces of Italian fascism; the conflict would be over in a matter of days. He was more concerned, in any case, to demonstrate to friends and foes his status as a full partner in the Rome-Berlin Axis, one who could pursue his own independent military campaign.

The Greek war, however, quickly proved to be the first in a series of unmitigated disasters for the Duce. Without ports to unload the troops or adequate mechanical and medical support, military leaders launched the invasion with a woefully insufficient force into mountainous terrain at the beginning of the rainy season. As a result, the Fascist offensive stalled in the first few days and a better trained and more determined Greek army counterattacked in early November. By the middle of the month, Italian commanders had little choice but to order a retreat, and in December the Greek military drove the invading troops back across the Albanian border. In the same month, disaster struck on the African front as well with the defeat of a large but poorly equipped Italian army by a much smaller mechanized British force in Libya, a defeat that presaged the loss of most of fascism's colonial empire in the spring of 1941. As a leading British diplomat commented sarcastically on the performance of the Italians in its aftermath, "Never had so much been surrendered by so many to so few."

While Mussolini attempted to blame these successive battlefield catastrophes on the incompetence of his military chiefs, the Fascist regime and its leader still suffered an irremediable loss of prestige and popularity on the home front. The best efforts of the Duce's propaganda machine could not mask the harsh realities of a war that so completely contradicted both the Italian public's expectations of a short, easy conflict and fascism's claims to military superiority and national greatness. Not only had the regime failed to establish Italy's supremacy in the Mediterranean by force, but it had proven itself incapable of defeating even lowly Greece or holding on to its few colonies in East Africa. These military setbacks completely overwhelmed Mussolini and his principal lieutenants, who had no alternative plan to restore popular morale, let alone to win back the hearts and minds of the Italian people. As the Duce admitted to one of his generals, "We are incapable of doing anything." Dramatic gestures designed to revive public confidence in the regime no longer seemed to work. His decision in January 1941 to send all of his ministers to fight on the Albanian front, for instance, succeeded only in antagonizing his closest collaborators and in further paralyzing government operations.

Mussolini recognized that Italy's "tragic situation" greatly reduced his freedom of action in foreign policy. As he conceded, "The only thing left to do is to place everything in Hitler's hands." The military debacles of the winter destroyed any illusions about pursuing an independent "parallel war" in the Mediterranean. In fact, the prospect of further setbacks made it imperative that he turn to his German allies for help. Hitler provided the help, but it came at a high price. From the beginning of 1941 onward, the Duce had to accept an explicitly subordinate position in his relationship with the Nazi leader. The steady influx of German troops into the Italian peninsula further underscored the country's growing subordination. As he bitterly observed, Italy was rapidly becoming little more than "a confederated province" of the Third Reich.

Mussolini's abject dependence on his Axis partner did produce immediate benefits in 1941, a year when Hitler appeared to be on the brink of winning the war. In March the German military spearheaded an offensive in North Africa that drove back the British army into Egypt and saved Italy's tenuous position in Libya. The following month Nazi forces came to the rescue of the besieged Italians in the Balkans, occupying Yugoslavia and imposing a surrender on the Greeks after a two-week campaign. In the aftermath, Hitler even allowed the Italians to govern parts of the newly conquered territories. These victories, however, were principally German triumphs that did not improve the image of the Fascist regime or rekindle confidence at home in the Duce's leadership. Moreover, reliance on the Nazis led Mussolini into a wider war against far more formidable adversaries in the second half of 1941. After the launching of Hitler's Operation Barbarossa in June, Mussolini dutifully committed Italy to fight the Soviet Union and insisted on sending Italian troops to the eastern front. Six months later, he joined Germany in declaring war on the United States after the Japanese attack on Pearl Harbor.

The disastrous consequences of these decisions became increasingly clear in the next year and a half. After a series of German advances in Russia and North Africa during the first half of 1942, the course of World War II turned decisively against the Axis powers. At the beginning of November, British tank units defeated the Italo-German army in Egypt at the Battle of El Alamein, and a week later Anglo-American forces launched a land campaign in Morocco and Algeria. In the same month, the Soviet army unleashed a counteroffensive against the Nazis on the eastern front at the Battle of Stalingrad. When that battle ended three months later, Germany had lost half a million men and any hope of achieving its new empire in the east. In February 1943, the Allies drove the Axis troops out of Libya, Italy's last remaining colony in Africa, foreshadowing their complete capitulation in North Africa in

May. By the summer of 1943, the Duce's "short war" had resulted in a death toll that included 205,000 Italian soldiers and 25,000 civilians.

Although these numbers paled in comparison with the losses suffered by Italy in the Great War, they had a devastating impact on a people who had reluctantly accepted this particular war in the first place. With Axis forces in retreat both in the east and in Africa, and Italian cities being hit by heavy allied bombardment, material conditions and popular morale began to collapse on the home front. Mounting shortages of coal and such essentials as bread, pasta, and oil compelled Mussolini to introduce severe rationing that put Italian food consumption on a par with that of Nazi-occupied Poland. Efforts to impose legal controls on the cost of living had little effect on prices and rents, which continued to soar at an alarming rate, while a thriving black market emerged to serve the rich. By the winter of 1942–1943, these conditions provoked growing discontent among most Italians, who now dreamed only of a quick end to the war.

The Duce's cult following melted away before the harsh realities of a losing war that he had imposed on his nation. Both foreign observers and police chiefs reported how his popularity within the Fascist party and among the Italian people plummeted as the war situation went from bad to worse. The king made the same point more bluntly when he informed Mussolini in the summer of 1943 that he had become "the most hated man in Italy."

Not surprisingly, Mussolini's physical and mental health began to deteriorate again as his sixtieth birthday approached. The Duce attempted to maintain his image as a virile exemplar of Fascist manhood by continuing his extramarital relationship with Clara Pettacci. He even embarked upon a new affair with a nineteen-year-old student, Elena Curti, in 1942. Nonetheless, he began to suffer increasingly from insomnia, colds, and severe stomach pains during the summer of that year. One of his ministers described Mussolini as "gray, ashy, with sunken cheeks, troubled and tired eyes," a man who seemed "not so much ill as humiliated, sad, and unable to struggle against his advancing years." In the following months, the pain intensified, he lost more than 40 pounds, and he was often unable to attend to his governmental responsibilities. An isolated and depressed Mussolini proved completely incapable of taking any effective measures as the military situation worsened in the winter of 1942–1943. When he did manage to rouse himself, he raged against the incompetence of his industrial, military, and political subordinates or else blamed the Italian people for having let him down. He stubbornly refused to consider any idea of a separate peace with the Allies, perhaps aware that they would demand his removal as a precondition for negotiations.

In this grim setting, fascism's respectable allies and moderate leaders began to take matters into their own hands, exploring the possibility of dumping their Duce in order to save the regime and their own positions of power. By the spring of 1943, the monarchy, the Vatican, and business leaders all favored a solution that would extract Italy from the war and forestall a revolutionary social crisis. A wave of strikes in the industrial centers of Milan and Turin in March, the first independent working-class demonstrations in nearly two decades, testified not only to mounting popular discontent, but also to an apparent resurgence of leftist militancy. At the same time, opposition to Mussolini grew within the Fascist party itself, especially after he dismissed some of his oldest and most prominent associates from the government in February. As the summer of 1943 approached, two separate groups of conspirators emerged at the highest levels of the regime: one in the court of Victor Emanuel III and the other involving a group of moderates on the Fascist Grand Council, headed by Dino Grandi and Giuseppe Bottai.

The catalyst for a decisive move by the two groups against Mussolini came in July. That month the war finally reached Italy with the landing of Anglo-American forces on the island of Sicily, followed by the bombardment of Rome on July 19. The immediate prospect of an Allied invasion of the Italian peninsula and the imminent collapse of the regime set in motion the events that led to the Duce's downfall. On July 16 Mussolini reluctantly complied with proposals from a contingent of party officials to convoke a meeting of the Fascist Grand Council, the first since 1939. During the meeting, which took place on the night of July 24–25, Grandi introduced a motion to limit the Duce's dictatorial powers and to restore sole command of the armed forces to the king. After a lengthy debate the motion passed by a vote of 19 to 7. An apathetic and exhausted Mussolini did not seem to understand the implications of what had occurred and chose not to have his supporters arrest the dissidents. Instead, he confidently informed the council that "the King is my friend, and I wonder what those who oppose me tonight will think tomorrow." The next day he returned to his normal work routine as if nothing had happened, before heading off to his regular consultation with the king. When he reported to Victor Emanuel about the vote, however, the king quietly informed Mussolini that he was removing him as head of government and replacing him with the monarchist general Pietro Badoglio, former commander-in-chief of the Italian armed forces. A small contingent of state police immediately placed the ex-Duce under arrest and whisked him off to a military hospital. With all the key centers of power in the hands of the army, the state radio announced on the evening of July 25 Mussolini's resignation, his replacement by Badoglio, and the king's resumption of military command.

The Fascist regime seemed to disappear with barely a whimper after Mussolini's removal and arrest. The fall of their Duce provoked no resistance from the rank and file in the Fascist party, militia, or youth organizations. Instead, the dramatic news of his political demise triggered spontaneous mass celebrations in Rome the next morning, with crowds rushing into the streets and public squares to tear down the symbols of the regime and voice their support for the monarchy. A few hard-liners like Roberto Farinacci sought asylum in the German embassy, but most prominent Fascists threw their support to Badoglio and the crown. For its part, the new government moved to distance itself from fascism by relying on apolitical career administrators to staff ministerial posts. In his confinement, the Duce learned firsthand of his abandonment from the chief of police, who reported: "The fascists have more than dispersed; they have vanished." As for public opinion, the same official told him, "There are innumerable demonstrations of hatred against you." Mussolini appeared ready to accept his fate and withdraw into obscurity in the summer of 1943. In response to the news from the chief of police, he conceded that his "star" had "fallen for ever." He even wrote a submissive note to Badoglio in late July, assuring him that he would "raise no difficulties of any sort" and "cooperate in every possible way."

However, the political career of Mussolini and Italian fascism did not end on July 25, 1943. Over the next month, the new government made a show of keeping Italy in the war on the side of the Axis while pursuing a negotiated settlement with the Allies. This strategy failed on both counts. On the one hand, Badoglio won no concessions from the Allies, who insisted on Italy's unconditional surrender as a prerequisite for any armistice. On the other hand, his government's assurances of continued loyalty to the Axis failed to fool the Germans. Hitler used the time wasted by the Italians in futile negotiations to rush military reinforcements onto the peninsula in preparation for Badoglio's anticipated desertion. When his government officially announced Italy's surrender and Allied forces landed on the southern mainland in early September, the Nazis swiftly occupied Rome and took control of most of the country north of the battlefront, forcing the king and his prime minister to abandon the capital and retreat to the south. A month later, the Badoglio government declared war on Germany.

This chaotic situation gave the Duce the illusion of a second lease on public life that would last for another 22 months. With the German army in control of much of the peninsula, Hitler decided to resurrect Mussolini from political oblivion, figuring that he was the only person with the stature to rally Fascist loyalists against the Badoglio regime and the Allies. The Nazi leader sent a glider team to rescue his Axis partner from captivity in a mountainous resort in central Italy in mid-September 1943 and installed him as the nominal leader of a German-sponsored Fascist state, the Italian Social Republic, based in the town of Salò, north of Milan. Mussolini went through the rituals of developing the new government's program, appointing a cabinet, and reorganizing the Fascist party and militia, but he remained essentially a symbolic leader who exercised little authority or control over events. The Duce and the Social Republic were, from the outset, creatures of the Nazi regime, which continued to make all the critical decisions and to dictate policy within the areas of Italy under German control. Only Japan and the smaller Axis satellite states officially recognized the puppet state. None of the neutral states, including the Vatican and Franco's Spain, gave it any diplomatic standing. Even German officials did not take their Italian Fascist ally very seriously. The chief of Nazi propaganda, Joseph Goebbels, dismissed the Social Republic as being so insignificant that it was "immaterial who occupies the various ministerial posts in Mussolini's cabinet."

A number of explanations have been advanced to explain the Duce's motives for agreeing to play such a humiliating role in a war that was rapidly deteriorating for the Axis. More sympathetic commentators later argued that he "put himself at the service of the nation" to protect the Italian people from the worst excesses of the Nazi occupation. Other interpretations have suggested that he did so in order to wreak revenge on the men who had betrayed him in July or else because he had rediscovered the socialist and republican ideals of his youth. The most compelling explanation, however, is that he really had little choice in the matter. Hitler fully intended to create a Fascist government in the north with or without his participation. By joining his old ally, Mussolini could hope for an eventual negotiated settlement of the war, from which he might emerge with some semblance of power and influence. The alternative seemed to offer no hope. If he accepted his fall from power and withdrew into private life, he still faced the prospect of eventual arrest, a public trial, imprisonment, even execution at the hands of the victorious Anglo-American forces.

Whatever his motives were for agreeing to head the Social Republic in the fall of 1943, Mussolini bears a heavy responsibility for the terror and violence carried out in its name during the ensuing months. To begin with, he gave a semblance of unity to the feuding groups that composed the puppet regime. His very presence at the head of the new state greatly increased its credibility and prestige in the eyes of misguided Italian patriots, young Fascist idealists, and the most fanatical elements of the party. He made matters worse by calling on his followers to launch a violent crusade against what he denounced as the "traitors" and "parasitical plutocrats" in Italy. Nor did he attempt to curb the excesses of Fascist extremists, who adopted the racial ideas and brutal methods of their Nazi patrons, and who gave the Social Republic its distinctively ferocious character. In this fashion, Mussolini contributed not only to the prolongation of the larger conflict, but also to the scale and intensity of the civil war and fratricidal violence that bloodied the Italian peninsula during the next 18 months.

The Social Republic displayed its extremism in its policies toward Italian Jews, antifascist resistance fighters, and the "traitors of July 25" who had voted for Mussolini's ouster. During the first years of the war, the Italian civilian and military authorities had done little to favor the racial policies of the Nazi regime in the territories under their control. Such obstructionism disappeared after the summer of 1943. At the behest of his German masters, Mussolini declared all Jews in the Social Republic enemy aliens, thereby clearing the way for the deportation of several thousand of them to Nazi extermination camps in Eastern Europe. Officials of the Social Republic also actively collaborated with the German authorities in the massacre of hostages and the public display of their corpses as reprisals against the antifascist resistance. Despite the desperate pleas of his favorite daughter, Edda, Mussolini even allowed his own son-in-law and former minister of foreign affairs, Galeazzo Ciano, and five other members of the Fascist Grand Council, to be executed for voting against him in the "*coup d'etat* of July 25."

Neither his rhetoric nor the violent excesses of the Social Republic revived the Duce's popularity or changed the course of the war on the Italian front. In June 1944, the city of Rome fell to Anglo-American forces who proceeded to sweep up the

peninsula. By the end of August, the Allies were
only 150 miles from Salò. As the military position of the German army deteriorated, the ranks
of the antifascist resistance steadily swelled in
northern Italy. Without an army or an independent government at his disposal, an ill, depressed,
and bitter Mussolini increasingly retreated into
his own fantasy world. During the brief respite
from hostilities in the winter of 1944–1945, he
talked about returning to the radical socialism of
his youth and taking revenge on the monarchy
and the old bourgeois allies whom he blamed for
the failures of fascism.

The harsh realities of the war forced Mussolini out of his reveries in April when the Allies
launched a final offensive in northern Italy. By
then the Duce had run out of options. The Nazis
rejected any idea of a Fascist government in exile
in Germany or of moving the capital of the Social Republic to the northeastern city of Trieste.
Abandoned by the rapidly disintegrating German regime, Mussolini talked boldly about how
"Fascism must die heroically," but he made no
effort to prepare a last stand of his followers in
the Alps. Instead, he moved to Milan the third
week in April in order to negotiate an end to
hostilities with the Allies and the political representatives of the Italian resistance movement.
With the cardinal archbishop of Milan acting as

mediator, he met with the partisans on the afternoon of April 25, but they offered him only unconditional surrender. When he learned that the German commander had already agreed to a separate armistice behind his back, Mussolini broke off negotiations, abandoned his family and the remaining loyalists of the Social Republic, and fled toward the border with Switzerland.

But the Duce's days were numbered. On the morning of April 27, 1945, a group of cars, containing the fallen leader, his mistress Clara Petacci, and a small number of top Fascist officials, joined a caravan of retreating German soldiers. Along the road, the convoy encountered a detachment of armed Italian partisans. After a brief exchange of fire, the partisans agreed to let the Germans pass if they turned over the Italians who accompanied them. A search of the caravan revealed the figure of Mussolini, dressed in a heavy German winter coat and helmet, hiding in the back of one of the trucks. He, his mistress, and several other Fascists were arrested and taken to a nearby farmhouse. On April 28, a group of Communist partisans arrived from Milan and removed Mussolini from the farm to a neighboring villa, where they summarily executed him and Petacci. The humiliating and disgraceful downfall of the man who less than a decade earlier had been glorified as the greatest

272 + BENITO MUSSOLINI

Italian of all ended with his death. The next day partisans transported Mussolini's and Petacci's corpses to Milan. There they were hung by the heels and put on display in Piazza Loreto, a public square in the center of the city, where crowds vented their anger and abuse on them.

X

The Duce's Legacy

Benito Mussolini's alliance with Nazi Germany, the humiliating defeats inflicted on his armies in World War II, and his ignominious death have largely shaped his much-diminished reputation since 1945. While his Axis partner, Adolf Hitler, continues to arouse fear and horror in the popular imagination, the Italian Fascist leader assumed a marginal place in the historical drama of the twentieth century, a figure more worthy of ridicule and disdain than dread. The close association between the two dictatorships in the public mind has inevitably evoked comparisons between the two leaders, in which Hitler completely overshadows Mussolini. Compared to Hitler, the Duce's relative lack of fanaticism, his limited use of political violence, the modesty of his accomplishments, and the smaller scale of his regime's crimes against humanity have made him appear as a lesser leader, one distinguished by his superficiality and incompetence.

The British historian A. J. P. Taylor captured this dominant view of the Duce in 1964 when he described him as a "vain, blundering boaster without either ideas or aims," who led a regime that was "corrupt, incompetent, and empty." The image of Mussolini as Hitler's clownish sidekick, windbag, and impostor has continued to dominate Anglo-American scholarship and popular accounts ever since. One of the Duce's most widely read biographers dismissed him in 1982 as a "gifted actor" whose only "superlative ability was as a propagandist," while another, more recent popular account depicted him as a "second-string Hitler, a wanna-be military genius, and, ultimately, a failed dictator." If Mussolini has made any lasting contribution, for most of his English-speaking commentators, it has been to the more shallow aspects of contemporary political culture in the west. Thus, they point to the seminal role he played in the development of our modern techniques of image building, myth making and "spin doctoring." The Duce and his regime pioneered such current staples of mass democracy as photo ops with sports heroes, artfully staged encounters with "the troops," and other choreographed public events designed to cultivate an emotional bond between leaders and their people.

While much of the western world has written Mussolini off as little more than a bad joke, he has had a more enduring impact in his homeland, where he has remained a lightning rod of political controversy in the years since his death. In the wake of World War II, he assumed a pivotal but overwhelmingly negative place in the official political culture of Italy's first republic. The new parliamentary democratic system that emerged from the ashes of war rested, in no small part, on a common rejection of all that Mussolini and his regime ostensibly stood for. Even in the worst years of the Cold War, communists, Catholics, and liberals could still unite in their shared antipathy to the fallen dictator and his regime. Not surprisingly, they presented him as something of a demonic figure who had imposed a criminal regime upon a reluctant Italian people. The image of the Duce advanced by the antifascist establishment highlighted his cultural poverty, the repressive nature of his dictatorship, and his lack of real achievements, as well as his singular responsibility for inflicting on his people the horrors of World War II.

The best efforts of a generation of political leaders and intellectuals did not prevent the memory of Mussolini from continuing to exercise a residual fascination among certain segments of Italian society. Although the new constitution officially outlawed the Fascist party, the Duce's hard-core loyalists maintained a political presence on the national scene after 1945 by means of another formation, the Italian Social Movement, which remained the country's fourth largest party in the ensuing decades. During the same period, the figure of Mussolini continued to evoke a certain nostalgia in southern Italy and in Italian emigrant communities abroad. Especially at times when corruption, inefficient public services, and disruptive strikes seemed to overwhelm the democratic state, some people in these areas fondly recollected the Fascist era as "good old days" of national glory and orderly government under the leadership of a "strong man."

In the past two decades, but especially after the end of the Cold War in the early 1990s, attempts by conservatives to soften the antifascist portrait of Mussolini have ensured that his legacy lives on in new controversies and debates within the Italian media and intellectual circles. Much as in the past, comparisons with Hitler have remained central to the image of the Fascist leader. Now, however, they have served as a means to define him as a "benign" dictator who relied less on terror than consensus to rule over his people, granted relatively greater personal freedom, treated his political opponents with comparative mildness, and avoided the atrocities of his German counterpart. As recently as the fall of 2003, Italy's Prime Minister Silvio Berlusconi echoed some of these themes in an interview with an English journalist that generated a firestorm of comment and criticism in the media. Asked to compare the Duce with Saddam Hussein, Berlusconi responded that the Iraqi dictator had caused millions of deaths, while "Mussolini never killed anyone," preferring instead to send his enemies "on holiday to internal exile." Most proponents of this view concede that the Fascist leader made some "mistakes," especially in his decisions to ally with Hitler and enter the Second World War, but they prefer to highlight the Duce's earlier popularity at home as well as his ostensible domestic achievements in constructing the first superhighways, crushing the Mafia, draining the swamps, and making peace with the Vatican. Such accounts of a "kinder and gentler" dictator have tended to neglect his responsibilities for the murder of political opponents, the massacres perpetrated by his regime in Ethiopia and Yugoslavia, the introduction of the Racial Laws, and the Republic of Salò's collaboration in the deportation of Jews from Italy after 1943.

If Mussolini remains a lightning rod for political controversy in his homeland, he has had perhaps his greatest, if unacknowledged, impact in the developing countries of the world where many of his ideas, techniques, and organizational innovations wound up influencing a generation of nationalist leaders and movements that came to prominence after 1945. Despite the enormous gap between rhetoric and accomplishments, Italian Fascism continued even after its demise to provide these new political forces with a vision and model of conservative revolution that promised both to restore order and to carry out rapid but controlled modernization of their societies. In the decade before World War II, the Duce and his regime attracted the admiration of a number of young army officers and political organizers from Latin America, the Middle East, and South Asia. After a stay in Rome, the future Argentine dictator Juan Peron came away greatly impressed by Mussolini's social reform programs and his skill in appealing to the masses. Similarly, the Brazilian political activist Plinio Salgado modeled his Integralist movement of 180,000 "green-shirts" on the example of fascism, following his visit to Italy in 1930.

During the same decade, Mussolini also encountered a favorable reception in the ranks of the anti-colonial movements within the British Empire. In India, he provided inspiration and direction to the leaders of right-wing Hindu nationalism, such as Subhas Chandra Bose and K. B. Hedgewar, founder of a youth movement, the

R.S.S. Members of the R.S.S. wore khaki uniforms and received paramilitary training and ideological indoctrination in accordance with the Fascist model. Likewise, Arab and Jewish extremists in the Middle East became open admirers of the Duce during the 1930s. These years saw the emergence of right-wing Arab imitations of fascism like the "Young Egypt" movement whose leader, Ahmed Hussain, claimed that Italy and Germany were "the only true democracies in Europe." At the same time, Ze'ev Jabotinsky, one of the key figures of right-wing Zionism and the founder of its youth movement, Betar, voiced public admiration for the Duce, mimicked his military style, and actively pursued his support. During the mid-1930s, a squadron of Betar recruits received training from the Black Shirts at the Italian naval academy at Civitavecchia, where they sang the Fascist party anthem, "Giovinezza." Men like Jabotinsky and the leaders of the Indian R.S.S. had largely disappeared from the public stage by the postwar era, but their disciples have continued to play leading roles in the political life of their respective countries.

Even the collapse of Italian fascism in World War II did not discourage a host of emerging nationalist leaders in the developing world from borrowing extensively from Mussolini's model to build or restructure their political systems after

1945. While openly Fascist movements failed to come to power in Latin America, both the Brazilian populist leader Getulio Vargas and the Argentine dictator Juan Peron adopted many of the trappings of fascism. Vargas' *Estado Novo*, for instance, paid implicit homage to the Duce's regime in its combination of right-wing nationalism, paternalistic social legislation, expanded internal markets, and repression of all independent working-class political movements. After he seized power in 1946, Peron also followed the example of Mussolini by mixing leftist and right-wing ideas and by creating his own cult of the personality, nourished by a mass movement, the Peronista party, and a mobilizing political hymn, "Muchachos Peronista."

The postwar years also saw the shadow of Mussolini in developments on the African continent and in the Middle East, where a generation of charismatic nationalist leaders began to set up populist parties and nationalist newspapers in order to mobilize mass support, especially among young people, against the colonial powers. After they had gained independence, many of these leaders used their personal prestige and power to forge new authoritarian regimes that, much like Italian fascism, combined repression with heavy doses of propaganda and leadership cults to deal with the challenges of nation building and modernization.

Kwame Nkrumah, for instance, constructed a single-party state with a command economy in Ghana after 1959. In rhetoric reminiscent of the cult of the Duce, his regime's propaganda glorified him as a "Man of Destiny" and his nation's "Redeemer." Nkrumah soon had himself proclaimed as Ghana's president for life, and his statues and photographs were displayed throughout the country to exalt his special status and leadership. In a similar vein, Middle Eastern dictatorships like those of Hafiz al-Asad in Syria and Saddam Hussein in Iraq combined state terror with personality cults that employed mass spectacles and other symbolic displays of power to engender obedience in their followers.

As these cases suggest, Mussolini's most enduring historical legacy in the twentieth century lies less in the scale of his accomplishments or in the conscious emulation of his regime than in the simple fact that he came first. Above all, he was the first of the dynamic new populist dictators to come to power and, as such, he ruled over the country in which fascism was invented. As a result, his regime provided the first great example to conservative elites and the middle classes elsewhere of how to achieve victory over the forces of revolution and "disorder" in the inter-war period. Although Hitler rapidly overshadowed his Axis partner on the international stage from the mid-1930s onward, the Nazi leader, along with a host of postwar dictators in the developing world, unavoidably imitated Mussolini in so far as they relied upon many of the political techniques and strategies he and his Black Shirts first developed and employed in the 1920s. Years before Hitler came to power, Mussolini was busy constructing an antiliberal and anticommunist regime based on a single mass party that combined repression of democracy with nationalist mobilization and ambitious social-welfare projects. In this fashion, the Duce emerged as the first of the twentieth-century dictators to rely not only on coercion, but also on new means of mass communications to consolidate his power and mobilize his people. His use of mass spectacle, film, radio, and photographic images to manufacture a cult of the charismatic leader who unified and inspired his country made him a global pioneer.

At the same time, Mussolini's career offers an object lesson on the limits of the politics of image and rhetorical extremism. From the Battle of Wheat for increased Italian grain production and the campaigns for "autarchy" to his welfare legislation, most of his social and economic innovations were either ineffectual or failed to live up to the expectations of their Fascist promoters. As events in the late 1930s and early 1940s illustrate, once the gap between image and reality became too great, the Duce's charismatic authority rapidly declined. When Mussolini and his regime demonstrated their weakness and incompetence in World War II, both his popular support at home and his international appeal evaporated. Postwar nationalist leaders elsewhere in the world may have adopted many of the Duce's techniques and methods, but none of them openly identified themselves and their states with the failed Italian dictator or his largely discredited Fascist ideology.

A Note on the Sources

Benito Mussolini has been the subject of more than a thousand profiles and biographies since he first emerged a national political figure in Italy before World War I. Nonetheless, the reputation of the Italian dictator continues to provoke intense debate and discussion, both in scholarly circles and in the popular press. Mussolini himself contributed greatly to the discord surrounding his historical legacy. He never provided a political vision or master plan comparable to Adolf Hitler's *Mein Kampf (My Struggle)*. Moreover, in a public career that spanned four decades and took him from revolutionary socialism to fascism, he expressed contradictory views on most of the great issues of the day. To further confuse matters, his private musings and actual policies often diverged from his public rhetoric and official pronouncements. The Duce provided abundant evidence of these contradictions and inconsistencies, since he was a prolific writer who repeatedly revised his own life story and whose collected works fill 44 volumes, edited by Eduardo and Duilio Susmel: *Opere omnia* (Florence: La Fenice, 1972–73), 37 vols., and *Opere omnia: Appendici* (Florence: Giovanni Volpe, 1978–80), 7 vols. As a result, students of his life have had a wealth of quotable materials with which to fashion interpretations of the Fascist dictator that fit their own intellectual or political preferences.

This book has relied heavily on the two most thorough treatments of the Duce's life: Renzo De Felice's *Mussolini* (Turin: Einaudi, 1965–97), 12 vols., and R. J. B. Bosworth's *Mussolini* (London: Arnold, 2002). Italy's leading historian of fascism, De Felice based his huge biography of Mussolini and the Fascist regime on an exhaustive examination of Italian public and private documents. It remains the basic reference point for all students working in the field. Although De Felice's interpretation evolved and changed over time, he increasingly portrayed the Fascist dictator as a visionary thinker committed to the long-term revolutionary transformation of the Italian people through the creation of a "new Fascist man." Bosworth's book, which provides a far more critical assessment of the Duce, is arguably the most complete biography of Mussolini currently available in any language. In his account, Mussolini emerges as a cynical misanthrope, crude

Darwinist, and opportunist who viewed politics as an arena for compromises and deals to achieve immediate tactical advantages that bolstered his own power and prestige.

I have also consulted a number of other biographical studies. Ivone Kirkpatrick's *Mussolini: A Study in Power* (New York: Avon, 1964) and Denis Mack Smith's *Mussolini* (New York: Knopf, 1982) offer richly detailed accounts of the Duce's political development and governmental policies. For more popularized accounts of Mussolini that include entertaining anecdotes from his life, students can consult Richard Collier, *Duce! A Biography of Benito Mussolini* (New York: Viking, 1971) and Alan Axelrod, *The Life and Work of Benito Mussolini* (Indianapolis: Alpha, 2002). Jaspar Ridley's *Mussolini* (New York: St. Martins Press, 1998) and Nicholas Farrell's *Mussolini: A New Life* (London: Weidenfeld and Nicholson, 2003) are recent efforts by journalists to provide a more sympathetic assessment of the Fascist dictator and his regime. A number of new biographies have appeared in Italy in the past decade, including Aurelio Lepre, *Mussolini l'italiano: Il Duce nel mito e nella realtà* (Milan: Mondadori, 1995); Alessandro Campi, *Mussolini* (Bologna: Il Mulino, 2001); Sergio Romano, *Mussolini: una biografia per immagini* (Milan: Longanesi, 2000);

and Marco Palla, *Mussolini e il fascismo* (Florence: Giunti, 1994). The Duce also has been the subject of a major biography by the French historian of Italian fascism, Pierre Milza: *Mussolini* (Paris: Fayard, 1999).

The battle to shape Mussolini's public image began early in his career, as Luisa Passerini shows in her *Mussolini immaginario: Storia di una biografia, 1915–1939* (Bari: Editori Laterza, 1991), a work that analyzes more than 400 biographies and profiles of the dictator before World War II. Mussolini offered descriptions and anecdotes from his childhood and adolescence in his *My Autobiography* (New York: Scribner, 1928) and in a series of interviews with the German journalist Emil Ludwig that were collected in *Talks with Mussolini* (London: Allen and Unwin, 1934). Gaudens Megaro's *Mussolini in the Making* (London: Allen and Unwin, 1938) remains an excellent source for Mussolini's early political career before the First World War. A. James Gregor advances an interpretation of the socialist phase of the Duce's career, *Young Mussolini and the Intellectual Origins of Fascism* (Berkeley: University of California Press, 1979), that stresses its continuities with Mussolini's subsequent reincarnation as a leader of fascism.

Three older studies, Christopher Seton-Watson's *Italy from Liberalism to Fascism: 1870–1925*

(London: Methuen, 1967); Adrian Lyttelton's *The Seizure of Power: Fascism in Italy, 1919–1929* (New York: Scribner, 1973); and Charles Maier's *Recasting Bourgeois Europe: Stabilization in France, Germany, and Italy in the Decade after World War I* (Princeton: Princeton University Press, 1975) provide a thorough introduction to the crisis of the Italian parliamentary state and the rise and triumph of Italian fascism in the 1920s. For the period from the March on Rome in 1922 to the consolidation of the dictatorship in 1925, in particular, students should consult Lyttelton's essay "Fascism in Italy: The Second Wave," in Walter Laqueur and George Mosse, eds., *International Fascism: 1920–45* (New York: Harper and Row, 1966).

A variety of works explore the creation and structure of Mussolini's totalitarian state. For thorough analyses of the institutions of the dictatorship, interested readers can consult Herman Finer, *Mussolini's Italy: A Classic Study of the Non-Communist One-Party State* (London: Gollancz, 1935), and Alberto Acquarone, *L'organizzazione dello stato totalitario* (Turin: Einaudi, 1965). Paul Corner's recent essay, "Italian Fascism: Whatever Happened to Dictatorship," *Journal of Modern History* (Vol.74, n.2, June 2002), examines the ways in which Mussolini employed the coercive instruments of a police state with more subtle mechanisms of social control to shape Italians' choices and attitudes toward the regime. Victoria De Grazia has authored two important studies of Mussolini's social policies: *The Culture of Consent: Mass Organization of Leisure in Fascist Italy* (Cambridge: Cambridge University Press, 1981) and *How Fascism Ruled Women: Italy 1922–1945* (Berkeley: University of California Press, 1992). The Fascist regime's welfare policies are the subject of Maria Sophia Quine's *Italy's Social Revolution: Charity and Welfare from Liberalism to Fascism* (London: Palgrave, 2002), while Carl Ipsen's fine study *Dictating Demography* (Cambridge: Cambridge University Press, 1996) explores the Duce's population policies. For a more detailed treatment of Fascist educational programs, readers should turn to Tracy H. Koon's *Believe, Obey, Fight: Political Socialization of Youth in Fascist Italy* (Chapel Hill: University of North Carolina Press, 1985).

In the past ten years, a younger generation of cultural historians, social scientists, and literary scholars have devoted systematic attention to Mussolini's role as a symbolic figure in Fascist rituals and ceremonies. Emilio Gentile pioneered a major revaluation of Fascist popular culture in his *The Sacralization of Politics in Fascist Italy* (Cambridge: Harvard University Press, 1996) and in his article "Mussolini's Charisma," *Modern*

Italy (n.3, 1996), which present fascism as a new secular religion in which the Duce became the all-knowing, omnipresent, all-powerful leader of the Italian people. Social scientists and cultural studies scholars have adopted a range of postmodern approaches that highlight aesthetics, rhetoric, ritual, and spectacle, as well as virility and "the body," as keys to understanding Mussolini's popular appeal. Readers interested in pursuing these themes should turn to Simonetta Falasca-Zamponi, *Fascist Spectacle: The Aesthetics of Power in Mussolini's Italy* (Berkeley: University of California Press, 1997); Barbara Spackman, *Fascist Virilities* (Minneapolis: University of Minnesota Press, 1996); Mabel Berezin, *Making the Fascist Self: The Political Culture of Inter-war Italy* (Ithaca: Cornell University Press, 1997); George Mosse, *The Image of Man: The Creation of Modern Masculinity* (New York: Oxford University Press, 1996). Two other important new studies of Fascist cultural practices, in which Mussolini does not feature as prominently, are Ruth Ben-Ghiat, *Fascist Modernities: Italy 1922–1945* (Berkeley: University of California Press, 2001), and Marla Stone, *The Patron State: Culture and Politics in Fascist Italy* (Princeton: Princeton University Press, 1998). Noteworthy earlier efforts to examine Fascist culture and the cult of the Duce include

Edward Tannenbaum's *The Fascist Experience: Italian Society and Culture, 1922–1945* (New York: Basic Books, 1972) and Piero Melograni's "The Cult of the Duce in Mussolini's Italy," *Journal of Contemporary History* (vol.II, 1976).

On the limits of the Duce's power, MacGregor Knox, *Common Destiny: Dictatorship, Foreign Policy and War in Fascist Italy and Nazi Germany* (Cambridge: Cambridge University Press, 2000), provides a lucid comparative analysis of the two Axis dictators, in which he identifies the ideological, institutional, and socioeconomic factors that restricted Mussolini's freedom of action and led him to compromise with representatives of the old order. For an introduction to Italy's economic development and problems in the Fascist era, students should read Vera Zamagni, *The Economic History of Italy, 1860–1990* (Berkeley: University of California Press, 1993), while Roland Sarti's *Fascism and the Industrial Leadership in Italy, 1919–1940: A Study in the Expansion of Power Under Fascism* (Berkeley: University of California Press, 1971) and his edited volume, *The Ax Within: Italian Fascism in Action* (New York: New Viewpoints, 1974), examine relations between the Duce and Italy's industrial elite. Ben-Ghiat's previously cited *Fascist Modernities* and David Forgacs, ed., *Rethinking Italian Fascism: Capitalism, Populism and Culture*

(London: Lawrence and Wishart, 1986), illuminate some of the cultural challenges that confronted Mussolini's regime.

A large body of scholarship exists on the Italian Fascist foreign policy. Allan Cassels, *Mussolini's Early Diplomacy* (Princeton: Princeton University Press, 1970), and H. James Burgwyn, *Italian Foreign Policy in the Inter-War Period, 1918–1940* (Westport, Conn.: Praeger, 1997), offer useful introductions to the subject. For Fascist colonial policies in Africa, Denis Mack Smith, *Mussolini's Roman Empire* (New York: Penguin, 1977), provides a highly readable account. MacGregor Knox's *Mussolini Unleashed, 1936–1941: Politics and Strategy in Fascist Italy's Last War* (Cambridge: Cambridge University Press, 1982) advances an interpretation of Mussolini as a revolutionary nationalist who embraced violence and war as instruments to forge a new national community at home and to elevate his country's power and prestige in the world. Similar views are propounded in three recent works: Robert Mallett, *Mussolini and the Origins of the Second World War, 1933–1940* (New York: Palgrave Macmillan, 2003); G. Bruce Strang, *On the Fiery March: Mussolini Prepares for War* (New York: Praeger, 2003); and Aristotle Kallis, *Fascist Ideology: Territory and Expansion in Italy and Germany, 1922–1945* (London:

Routledge, 2000). For additional information on the Duce's anti-Jewish policies and Fascist occupation policies during the war, readers can consult Enzo Collotti, ed., *Fascismo e antifascismo: Rimozioni, revisioni, negazioni* (Rome: Laterza, 2000); Michele Sarfatti, *Gli ebrei nell'Italia fascista: Vicende, identità* (Turin: Einaudi, 2000); and Davide Rodogno, *Il nuovo ordine mediterraneo: Le politiche di occupazione dell'Italia fascista in Europa (1940–1943)* (Turin: Bollati Boringhieri, 2003). Finally, Robert O. Paxton's *The Anatomy of Fascism* (New York: Knopf, 2004) offers a useful examination of Mussolini's legacy and influence in the developing world since the 1930s.

Glossary

Acerbo Law: The majority electoral law of 1923 that permitted the Fascists to control parliament by giving two-thirds of the 535 seats in the Chamber of Deputies to the electoral list with the largest number of votes.

Arditi: Italy's assault troops in World War I. After the war, some Arditi formed the *Fasci di Combattimento* with Mussolini.

Avanti!: National daily newspaper of the Italian Socialist Party. Mussolini was editor of the paper between 1912 and the fall of 1914.

Aventine Secession: Group of 150 antifascist deputies who abandoned the Chamber of Deputies to protest the murder of Matteotti.

Badoglio, Pietro: Army chief of staff from 1925 to 1940 and Mussolini's successor as head of government after July 1943.

Battle of Guadalajara: Major military setback and political humiliation for Mussolini and the Fascist regime during the Spanish Civil War in 1937.

Black Shirts: The term applied to devoted followers of the Fascist movement who wore black shirts as part of their uniform.

Catholic Action: The lay Catholic organization that remained one of the few independent organizations in Italy after 1929. It competed with the Fascist regime in the areas of youth education and leisure activities in the 1930s.

Confindustria: Organization of Italian industrial employers that played a major role in shaping economic policy and labor relations during the Fascist era.

Corporatism: The Fascist system governing relations between capital and labor, in which the two sides were integrated into obligatory, hierarchical corporations, recognized by the state as organs of self-regulation within each sector of production. The corporative system in Italy remained largely an artificial bureaucratic structure without independent initiative and with little control over employer associations.

Cult of the Duce: The product of a multimedia campaign of the Fascist regime to promote an idealized image of Mussolini as the all-knowing, heroic, and superhuman leader who was shaping Italy's destiny.

Ethiopian War: The Fascist invasion of the African country of Ethiopia in October 1935 that ended in May 1936 with the occupation of the country's capital, Addis Ababa. The war marked a major shift in Italian foreign policy and ushered in changes in Mussolini's relations with the western democracies and Nazi Germany.

Fiume Expedition: The occupation in September 1919 of the disputed city of Fiume, on the border between Italy and Yugoslavia, by veteran volunteers led by the writer and interventionist leader Gabriele D'Annunzio. The Expedition undermined the authority of the Italian government and prefigured Mussolini's March on Rome.

Fascio di Combattimento: The earliest organizational unit of Italian fascism. The first fascio was founded in Milan on March 21, 1919.

Fascist Grand Council: Originally created as a consultative body of the Fascist party, the Grand Council became the highest organ of the Italian state and the Fascist regime. In 1943 it provided the setting for the overthrow of Mussolini.

Franco, Francisco: Leader of the Nationalist cause against the Spanish Republic in July 1936 and the recipient of substantial material and military support from the Fascist regime.

Futurists: Members of the first major Italian arts movement of the twentieth century. Futurism violently rejected the past and celebrated modern life. One of the key figures in the movement, F. T. Marinetti, and other members joined with Mussolini in 1919.

Giolitti, Giovanni: The most important Italian statesman of Italy before World War I. Giolitti helped pave the way for the Fascist seizure of power through his miscalculations and misjudgments in the postwar years.

***Il Popolo d'Italia*:** The daily newspaper founded by Mussolini in November 1914 as a force for Italian intervention in World War I. The paper became the official organ of the Fascist regime after 1922.

Interventionist Cause: Movement consisting of a wide variety of political and ideological groups in support of Italian intervention in World War I. Mussolini contributed to the campaign by glorifying the use of violence in mass rallies.

IRI (Institute for Industrial Reconstruction): The para-state agency founded in 1933 to deal with the world-wide economic depression by purchasing all shares of stocks previously held by Italian banks. As a result of IRI, the Italian government controlled a proportionally larger share of national industry than any other government in Europe except the Soviet Union by 1939.

Italian Social Republic: Mussolini's government in northern Italy between September 1943 and April 1945. This government was little more than a puppet regime of Nazi Germany.

Lateran Accords: Pacts signed in February 1929 by the Papacy and the Fascist government that enormously enhanced Mussolini's prestige and popularity in the Catholic world but undermined the totalitarian pretensions of his regime by granting the Church a privileged position in Italy.

March on Rome: The projected military occupation of Italy's capital by the Fascist squads in October 1922. The march was the central event in a larger crisis of public order and parliamentary government that culminated in Mussolini's accession to power.

Matteotti Affair: One of the critical moments in the history of fascism, the kidnapping and murder of Giacomo Matteotti, a Socialist deputy, in June 1924 opened a crisis that ended with the imposition of the Fascist dictatorship the following year.

Munich Conference: A conference of the leaders of Great Britain, France, Germany, and Italy in September 1938, in which Mussolini mediated the crisis provoked by Hitler's territorial demands in Czechoslovakia. The capitulation of the western democracies at the conference convinced the Duce of their weakness and the wisdom of allying with Nazi Germany.

ONMI (National Institute for Maternity and Infancy): Established in 1925, ONMI was one of the first institutions of the Fascist regime designed to strengthen the Italian family by supervising children's and mothers' welfare.

Opera Nazionale Balilla: The Fascist youth organization for boys ages 8 to 14, founded in 1926 to mobilize the support of young people for the regime.

Opera Nazionale Dopolavoro: The Fascist after-work organization for workers, peasants, and salaried employees, founded in 1925. Its activities encompassed virtually everything associated with mass culture.

OVRA: The special police force devoted to repressing clandestine enemies of the Fascist regime.

Pact of Steel: The political and military alliance signed in Berlin in May 1939 between Nazi Germany and Fascist Italy that gave Hitler a virtual free hand in the pursuit of his expansionist goals.

Punitive Expeditions: Violent assaults by Fascist paramilitary groups against the Socialist movement in northern and central Italy, especially in the years between 1920 and 1922.

Racial Laws: Series of anti-Semitic decrees in 1938 that forbade intermarriage between Italians and Jews, removed Jews from positions of influence in the government and professions, and restricted their property holdings.

Ras: The paramilitary bosses of provincial fascism. The ras rose to prominence during the armed terrorist offensive against the socialist labor movement in 1921. They derived their name from the term for Ethiopian chieftains.

Rome-Berlin Axis: Term coined by Mussolini in November 1936 to describe the growing ideological, personal, political, and ultimately military alliance with Adolf Hitler and Nazi Germany.

Spanish Civil War: The war in Spain between 1936 and 1939, in which Mussolini intervened in the hopes of establishing a conservative authoritarian regime that would strengthen Italian influence in the western Mediterranean. The war exposed the military weakness of the Fascist regime, further poisoned relations with the western democracies, and strengthened ties with Nazi Germany.

Special Tribunal for the Defense of the Fascist State: Military tribunal set up in 1927 to try and punish individuals charged with antifascist activities and crimes against the state.

Squadristi: The armed fighting force of fascism. The squadristi represented the most distinctive and innovative feature of the movement and played a decisive role in the emergence of Mussolini as a major political force before 1922.

Victor Emanuel III: The king of Italy from 1900 until his abdication in 1946. Victor Emanuel III played a crucial role in Mussolini's rise to power and in the Duce's downfall in 1943. Despite personal reservations, the king approved all the major decisions and policies of the Fascist regime.

Vidoni Palace Agreement: Agreement between Confindustria and the Fascist union organizations in 1925 that marked a major victory for both fascism and the industrialists at the expense of the workers. According to its terms, non-fascist unions were excluded from labor negotiations and the authority of management over the factories was guaranteed by the state.

Photo Credits

p. ii: Hulton Archive/Getty Images

p. 3: Bettmann/Corbis

p. 19: *(top left)* Time Life Pictures/Getty Images;
      (center and top right) Hulton Archive/Getty Images

p. 73: Bettmann/Corbis

p. 104: Alinari/Art Resource, NY

p. 128: Hulton Archive/Getty Images

Index